Air Fryer
Cookbook for Beginners
Amazingly Easy Recipes to Fry, Bake, Grill, and Roast with Your Air Fryer

OLIVIA WOOD

Text Copyright © Olivia Wood

All rights reserved. No part of this guide may be reproduced in any form without permission in writing from the publisher except in the case of brief quotations embodied in critical articles or reviews.

Legal & Disclaimer

The information contained in this book and its contents is not designed to replace or take the place of any form of medical or professional advice; and is not meant to replace the need for independent medical, financial, legal or other professional advice or services, as may be required. The content and information in this book has been provided for educational and entertainment purposes only.

The content and information contained in this book has been compiled from sources deemed reliable, and it is accurate to the best of the Author's knowledge, information and belief. However, the Author cannot guarantee its accuracy and validity and cannot be held liable for any errors and/or omissions. Further, changes are periodically made to this book as and when needed. Where appropriate and/or necessary, you must consult a professional (including but not limited to your doctor, attorney, financial advisor or such other professional advisor) before using any of the suggested remedies, techniques, or information in this book.

Upon using the contents and information contained in this book, you agree to hold harmless the Author from and against any damages, costs, and expenses, including any legal fees potentially resulting from the application of any of the information provided by this book. This disclaimer applies to any loss, damages or injury caused by the use and application, whether directly or indirectly, of any advice or information presented, whether for breach of contract, tort, negligence, personal injury, criminal intent, or under any other cause of action.

You agree to accept all risks of using the information presented inside this book.

You agree that by continuing to read this book, where appropriate and/or necessary, you shall consult a professional (including but not limited to your doctor, attorney, or financial advisor or such other advisor as needed) before using any of the suggested remedies, techniques, or information in this book.

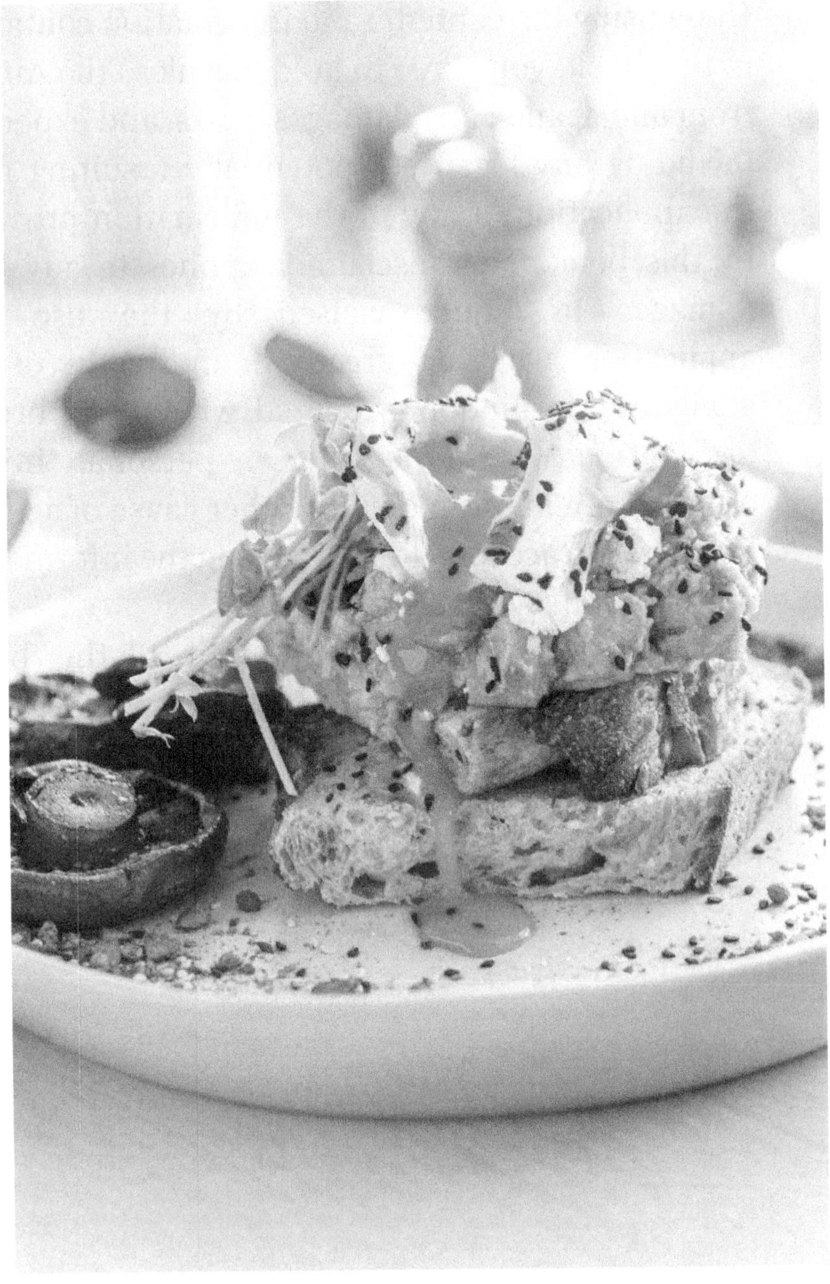

Table of Contents

Description 9
Introduction 10
Breakfast Recipes 17

Blueberry Cream Cheese with French Toast 18
Bread Cups Omelette 20
Air Fried Potato Pancakes 22
Exquisite Dutch Pancake 24
Clean Breakfast Sandwich 26
Craving Cinnamon Toast 28
Wow! Feta Breakfast 30
Cinnamon Flavored Grilled Pineapples 32
The Great Japanese Omelette 34
Air Fried Hashbrown 36
Breakfast Turkey Melt Sandwich 38
Deserving Cheesy Omelette 40
Air Fried Cheese Soufflé 42
Chicken and Potato Nuggets 46
Herbed Cauliflower Quinoa and Cheese Casserole 48
Home-made Sausage Frittata 50
Herbed Sweet Potato Hash 52

Spinach Frittata with Cherry Tomato and Cheddar 54
Herbed Salmon and Cheese Frittata 56
Asparagus & Bacon Spears 58
Tender Potato Pancakes 60
Bacon Egg Muffins 62
Air Fryer Baked Cheesy Eggs 64
Air Fried Mac & Cheese 66

Main Dish 69

Roasted Salmon with Lemon and Rosemary .. 70
Air Fried Meatballs with Parsley 72
Succulent Flank Steak 74
Chili Roasted Eggplant Soba 76
Quinoa and Spinach Cakes 78
Air Fried Cajun Shrimp 80
Air Fried Squid Rings 82
Marinated Portabello Mushroom 84
Air Fried Meatloaf 86
Fettuccini with Roasted Vegetables in Tomato Sauce 88
Herbed Parmesan Turkey Meatballs 90
Teriyaki Glazed Salmon and Vegetable Roast. 92
Sirloin with Garlic and Thyme 94
Air Fried Chicken Tenders with Honey Mustard Dip 96

Fish and Lentil Burger Patties 98
Korean Style Chicken Thighs 100
Almond Crusted Chicken Fingers 102
Roast Pork Loin with Red Potatoes 104
Beef Zucchini Patties with Feta Cheese 106
Portobello Pizza 108
Bacon Wrapped Chicken 110
Air fried Fish Cakes 112
Turkey Meatballs 114
Air Fryer Baked Garlic Parsley Potatoes 116
Roasted Chicken Breast and Vegetables 118
Roasted Green Beans with Shrimp 120
Air-fried Chicken Skewers 122
Rosemary Lamb Chops 124
Grilled Steak with Red Onion and Tomatoes ..126
Chicken Bruschetta 128
Air Fryer Cajun Tuna Steaks 130
Walnut-Crusted Pork Chops 132
Cheese Almond Stuffed Tenderloin 134
Baked Tilapia with Parmesan 136
Zucchini, Tomato and Mozzarella Pie 138
Chicken with Tomato Mixture 140

Appetizers **143**

Breaded Jalapeno Poppers 144

Sweet Potato Fries with Basil 146
Red Pepper Bites with Mozzarella 148
Air Fried Tofu with Peanut Dipping Sauce 150
Tuna and Potato Croquettes 152
Beef and Vegetable Samosas 154
Air-Fried Mozzarella Sticks with Sesame Seeds 156
Zucchini Wedges with Marinara Sauce 158
Cod Fritters with Chives 160
Spiced Potato Chip with Garlic Yogurt Dip 162

Desserts/Snacks **165**

Bruschetta with Pesto Cheese and Tomato 166
Air Fried Pumpkin Chips 168
Cheesy Bacon Fries 170
Apple Cinnamon Crumble with Almond 174
Peach with Cinnamon Dessert 176

Conclusion **178**

Description

Have you ever tried the many different ways you can make tasty foods in your Air Fryer? Not only will these foods be delicious, but they will contain fewer calories and be healthier for you! The recipes are easy to make and easy to follow. You will absolutely love how quick and effortless it is to cook with an Air fryer, and how tasty, fresh, and delicious your food will be if you follow the recipes in this book

This innovation makes it possible to enjoy fried foods with less oil. You can also use it to whip up a wide range of dishes, snacks, and desserts.

It features loads of recipes that you can tweak in many ways to suit your preference and the availability of ingredients. Each recipe has a nutrient content guide per serving.

With an air fryer, it takes less time to cook, and you can cook just about anything! Your meals will have less calories and less cholesterol than traditional recipes. Cooking with an Air Fryer is a win-win situation, and this book will tell you how to create delicious meals quickly and easily.

Keep on reading to learn everything you need to know about using an Air Fryer, so you can start to create delicious meals with less grease and more flavor!

Introduction

The technology used in air fryers is called "Rapid Air Technology" which causes the heat to be pushed by a rapidly turning fan. Ovens, unless they are convection style, do not have fans that constantly circulate the heat. Air fryers have a removable basket in which the food sits, and the hot air circulates all around to cook the food.

One of the most popular things to make in an air fryer is French fries. These tasty treats are normally submerged in a vat full of oil and are dep fried at high heat. The potatoes soak up quite a bit of the oil and retain it, and it is consumed. We all know that oil is not necessarily good for the body. Some oils cause plaque to form in our blood vessels and encumber our bodies with extra fat. If you reduce the amount of oil and the food tastes great, how can you go wrong?

What Can be prepared In An Air Fryer?
You can cook anything you would normally deep fry: French fries, fried chicken, fried fish, and all those other unhealthy foods cook up great in an air fryer and are safer to eat. But that is not all you can do in an air fryer. I make scrambled eggs for breakfast or French Toast. I can cook up empanadas or Chinese dumplings for my lunch.

It isn't hard to make meatloaf, pork chops, salmon, country fried steak, or BBQ chicken in the air fryer. As long as the dish isn't liquid, like soup or stew, it is a possibility in an air fryer. It is also able to make a cake, hand pies, and other desserts in the air fryer. The basket of the air fryer has little slits in it so that the air can flow through. Some things I make in my air fryer are not suitable to put in that basket because it would leak all over. To remedy that, you can use a small 4 to 6 inch metal cake pan, ceramic ramekins, or small metal bowl with a flat bottom to put things in too cook, a process I use to cook my scrambled eggs in the morning. Some air fryers even come with an accessory like this to put in the basket. This makes for so many more possibilities when it comes to meals you can make in an air fryer.

Is Food Really Healthier When Made In An Air Fryer?

The fan in the air fryer not only circulates hot air around the food, but it also circulates out droplets of oil and creates a chemical reaction called The Mallard Effect. This effect causes the food to turn brown and crispy and adds some flavor to the food. Air fried foods contain much less fat, but they taste is about the same, and sometimes even better. Fried chicken made in an air fryer contains about the same amount of fat as a roasted or baked chicken.

Not only do foods contain less fat, but they also have fewer calories. When food is fried, a compound is created on the food that we consume. This substance is acrylamide, and it is thought to be a carcinogen (cancer-causing).

A study was performed, and it was found that the acrylamide content was reduced by 90% when food was cooked in an air fryer. I have an issue with loving fried foods too much. I eat them, and that results in terrible heart burn and stomachs aches. I can eat fries and other fried foods in the air fryer with no effect. I can say with certainty because of my own weight loss that foods made in an air fryer are healthier for me.

Benefits

- Food is healthier because oil use is greatly reduced. Still, everything comes out crispy and brown that is supposed to.
- Food cooks quicker and more efficently. Heat does not escape from the air fryer like it does on a cooktop or oven. It takes less time to cook or reheat food because it stays in the air fryer and circulates.
- The air fryer is more efficient. Because the heat stays in the unit and does not vent, it cooks more efficiently and faster without using as much electricity. I hate turning my oven on in the summer because it heats up the house.

Not so with an air fryer. the heat created in the air fryer stays in the air fryer.
- It is versatile, and you can make a variety of foods ranging from breakfast items to mouth-watering desserts.
- Most units are small and fit on the counter top or in a cupboard for storage
- They are quite easy to clean, with lots of detahcable parts and components that can be placed in the dish washer.
- Heating up frozen foods that would normally go in an oven at high temperature can be cooked in a matter of minutes including chicken tenders and nuggets, fish sticks and frozen fries.

Accessories

Some air fryers come with accessories, and they include:
- Racks that go inside the basket
- Grill pan
- Baking dish
- Steamer
- Silicone pan or cups
- Rubber ended tongs that do not scratch

It is worth getting the silicone pan or cups, steamer and baking dish, and absolutely necessary to get rubber ended tongs.

Don't try removing food from the basket with a fork because you will scratch the surface of the basket and everything will stick in the future.

The 6-inch basket fits perfectly into the air fryer with a little room to fit the rubber tipped tongs in to get it out. The 4-inch basket is perfect for making single serve omelets, or you can use a ramekin.

Tips

The following tips will help you make the best of your air fryer:

- I suggest preheating your air fryer before putting anything in it. Not all recipes call for this, but I do it anyway. I set the fryer for the temperature stated in the recipe and cook the food 1 to 4 minutes. The bigger the item is that goes in, the longer I preheat. If I am cooking a few fries, I preheat 1 or 2 minutes, and if I am cooking two chicken breasts, I would preheat 4 minutes. I also preheat a little longer if the food being placed in the air fryer is frozen. If I make my own chicken nuggets, I preheat for 2 minutes. If I am doing frozen chicken nuggets, I preheat 4 minutes.
- Many recipes require cooking spray to be sprayed on the food, so make sure you have a variety including butter flavored and olive or canola oil types. I actually prefer a kitchen pump spray bottle that allows me to put olive oil and other oils in to spray.

- When breading items to be air fried, it is important to dredge in flour first and then press the breadcrumbs into the meat. The fan puts out a lot of power and will blow the breadcrumbs off if you don't do it right.
- Putting a tablespoon or so of water in the drawer that holds the basket will stop greasy foods like bacon or ham from causing smoke to appear
- Secure tops of sandwiches with toothpicks and cut them down just above the food they are holding. The air fryer fan is very powerful and often lifts the top bread from a sandwich while cooking.
- Never overcrowd the basket because the food will not get cooked evenly or properly. Everything must be in a single layer and not overlapping.
- Flip most items cooked in the air fryer half way through the time allotted for cooking. This allows the food to cook evenly. Of course, there will be some things you can't do this with.
- Always check meat and other foods that could give you food poisoning with an instant-read thermometer to make sure it is really done. If it does not meet requirements for that food, put it back in and cook it a little longer (maybe 1 or 2 minutes) and check again. This is especially necessary when cooking frozen foods.

- If you use a light weight cake pan or metal bowl in your air fryer, do not be concerned if it makes a lot of noise. The fan is going to push it around in there, and you will hear it clanging especially if there isn't much in there. To make scrambled eggs, you must air fry the butter in a pan while you are preheating the air fryer and it will clang around for the whole 2 minutes it is preheating. Once you put the eggs in, it weights it down, and it will no longer move around or make noise.

Now it is time to get cooking with your air fryer. Remember to always check while cooking because all air fryers do not cook at the same temperatures and times. Start with breakfast and make your way to snacks, desserts. and cooking readymade items.

Breakfast Recipes

Blueberry Cream Cheese with French Toast

Servings: 4

Ingredients

- 2 eggs, beaten
- 4 slices bread
- 3 tsps. sugar
- 1½ c. corn flakes
- 1/3 c. milk
- ¼ tsp. nutmeg
- 4 tbsps. berry-flavored cheese
- ¼ tsp. salt

Directions

1. Pre-heat your Air Fryer to 400 degrees F.
2. In a medium bowl, mix sugar, eggs, nutmeg, salt and milk.
3. In a separate bowl, mix blueberries and cheese.
4. Take 2 bread slices and gently pour the blueberry mixture over the slices. Top with the milk mixture. Cover with the remaining two slices to make sandwiches. Dredge the sandwiches over cornflakes to coat well.
5. Lay the sandwiches in your air fryer's cooking basket and cook for 8 minutes.
6. Serve with berries and syrup.
7. Enjoy!

Nutritional Information:

Calories: 428
Fat: 11.3g
Carbs: 53.7g
Protein: 23.4g

Bread Cups Omelette

Servings: 4

Ingredients

- 4 crusty rolls
- 5 eggs, beaten
- Pinch salt
- ½ tsp. dried thyme
- 3 strips precooked bacon, chopped
- 2 tbsps. heavy cream
- 4 Gouda or Swiss cheese mini wedges, thin slices

Directions

1. Preheat your air fryer 330 degrees F.
2. Chop off the rolls' tops and get rid of the inside with your fingers.
3. Line a slice of cheese to the rolls and gently press down, so the cheese conforms to the inside of the roll.
4. In a medium-sized bowl, mix eggs with heavy cream, bacon, thyme, salt, and pepper.
5. Stuff the rolls with the egg mixture.
6. Lay the rolls in your air fryer's cooking basket and bake for 8 to 12 minutes or until the eggs become puffy and the roll shows a golden brown texture.
7. Enjoy!

Nutritional Information:

Calories: 499
Fat: 24g
Carbs: 46g
Protein: 26g

Air Fried Potato Pancakes

Servings: 4

Ingredients

- 200g potatoes, cleaned and peeled
- 1 chopped onion
- 1 egg, beaten
- ¼ c. low-fat milk
- 2 tbsps. unsalted butter
- ½ tsp. garlic powder
- ¼ tsp. Kosher salt
- 3 tbsps. all-purpose flour
- ground black pepper

Directions:

1. Shred the peeled potatoes and then transfer in a bowl filled with cold water to wash off excess starch.
2. Drain the potatoes and the use of paper towels to dry off the potatoes.
3. In a mixing bowl, combine together egg, butter, garlic powder, salt and pepper, and lastly the flour. Stir well. Add in shredded potatoes.
4. Preheat Air Fryer to 390°F.
5. Pull out the Air Fryer cooking basket and then place ¼ cup of the potato pancake batter in the cooking basket.
6. Cook until golden brown for approximately 10 minutes.
7. Serve and enjoy!

Nutritional Information:

Calories: 255
Fat: 8.4 g
Carbs: 42 g
Protein: 7.1 g

Exquisite Dutch Pancake

Servings: 4

Ingredients

- 3 eggs, beaten
- 2 tbsps. unsalted butter
- ½ c. flour
- 2 tbsps. powdered sugar
- ½ c. milk
- 1½ c. freshly sliced strawberries

Directions

1. Preheat your Air Fryer to 330 degrees F.
2. Set a pan on low heat and melt butter.
3. In a medium-sized bowl, mix flour, milk, eggs, and vanilla until fully incorporated. Add the mixture to the pan with melted butter.
4. Place the pan in your air fryer's cooking basket and bake for 12-16 minutes until the pancake is fluffy and golden brown.
5. Drizzle powdered sugar and toss sliced strawberries on top.
6. Serve and enjoy!

Nutritional Information:

Calories: 196
Fat: 9g
Carbs: 19g
Protein: 16g

Clean Breakfast Sandwich

Servings: 1

Ingredients

- 1 whole egg
- 1 slice English bacon
- Salt and pepper
- 1 slice bread
- ½ c. butter

Directions

1. Preheat your Air Fryer to 400 degrees F.
2. To one side of the bread slice, apply butter. Add the cracked egg on top and season with salt and pepper.
3. Place bacon on top.
4. Place the bread slice in your Air Fryer's cooking basket and bake for 3-5 minutes.
5. Serve and enjoy!

Nutritional Information:

Calories: 320
Fat: 13g
Carbs: 33g
Protein: 17g

Craving Cinnamon Toast

Servings: 6

Ingredients

- 12 slices bread
- Pepper
- ½ c. sugar
- 1 stick butter
- 1½ tsps. vanilla extract
- 1½ tsps. cinnamon

Directions

1. Preheat your Air Fryer up to 400 degrees F.
2. In a microwave proof bowl, mix butter, pepper, sugar and vanilla extract. Warm the mixture for 30 seconds until everything melts as you stir.
3. Pour the mixture over bread slices.
4. Lay the bread slices in your air fryer's cooking basket and cook for 5 minutes.
5. Serve with fresh banana and berry sauce.
6. Enjoy!

Nutritional Information:

Calories: 81
Fat: 5g
Carbs: 8g
Protein: 3g

Wow! Feta Breakfast

Servings: 3

Ingredients

- 3½ lbs. feta cheese
- Pepper
- 1 whole chopped onion
- 2 tbsps. chopped parsley
- 1 egg yolk
- Olive oil
- 5 sheets frozen filo pastry

Directions

1. Preheat your Air Fryer to 400 degrees F.
2. Cut each of the 5 filo sheets into three equal sized strips.
3. Cover the strips with olive oil.
4. In a bowl, mix onion, pepper, feta, salt, egg yolk, and parsley.
5. Make triangles using the cut strips and add a little bit of the feta mixture on top of each triangle.
6. Place the triangles in your air fryer's cooking basket and cook for 3 minutes.
7. Serve alongside green onions and a drizzle of olive oil.
8. Enjoy!

Nutritional Information:

Calories: 426
Fat: 14g
Carbs: 65g
Protein: 9g

Cinnamon Flavored Grilled Pineapples

Servings: 2

Ingredients

- 1 tsp. cinnamon
- 5 pineapple slices
- ½ c. brown sugar
- 1 tbsp. chopped basil
- 1 tbsp. honey

Directions

1. Preheat your air fryer to 340 degrees F.
2. Using a bowl, combine cinnamon and brown sugar.
3. Drizzle the sugar mixture over your pineapple slices and set aside for about 20 minutes.
4. Place the pineapple rings in the air fryer cooking basket and cook for 10 minutes. Flip the pineapples and cook for 10 minutes more.
5. Serve with basil and a drizzle of honey.

Nutritional Information:

Calories: 480
Fat: 18g
Carbs: 71g
Protein: 13g

The Great Japanese Omelette

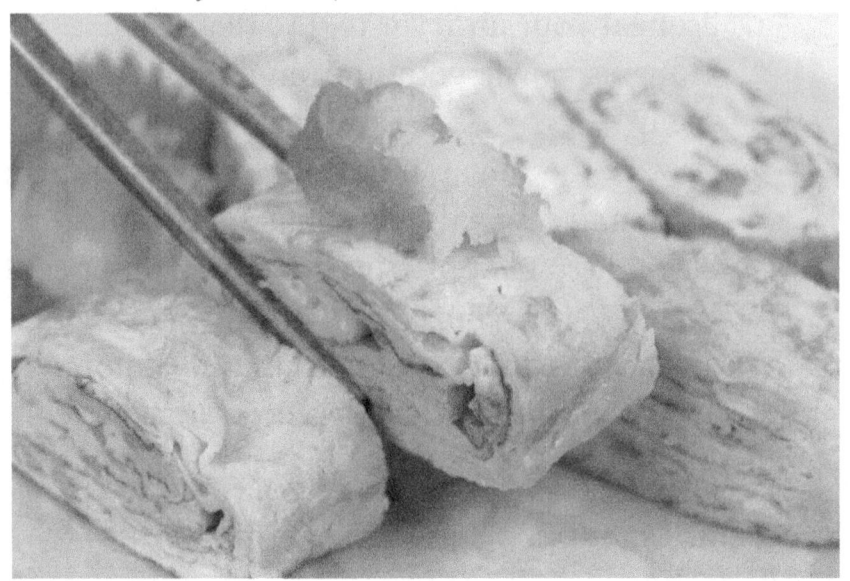

Servings: 1

Ingredients

- 1 cubed Japanese tofu
- 3 whole eggs
- Pepper
- 1 tsp. coriander
- 1 tsp. cumin
- 2 tbsps. soy sauce
- 2 tbsps. chopped green onion
- Olive oil
- 1 chopped onion

Directions

1. Preheat your Air Fryer up to 400 degrees F.
2. Using a medium bowl, mix eggs, soy sauce, pepper, oil, and salt.
3. Add cubed tofu to baking forms and pour the egg mixture on top.
4. Place the prepared forms in the air fryer cooking basket and cook for 10 minutes.
5. Serve with a sprinkle of herbs.
6. Enjoy!

Nutritional Information:

Calories: 300
Fat: 40g
Carbs: 19g
Protein: 72g

Air Fried Hashbrown

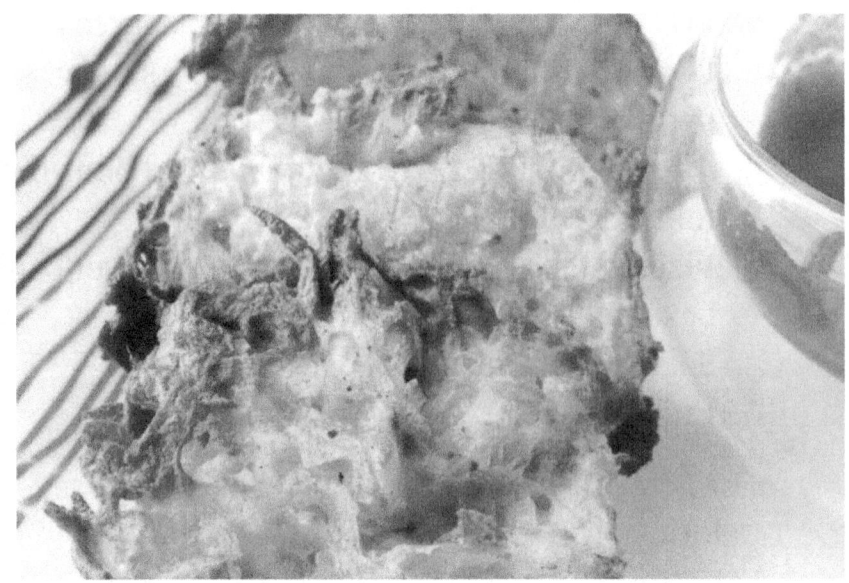

Servings: 4

Ingredients

- 4 (200g) potatoes, cleaned and peeled
- 3 tbsps. butter, melted
- ½ tsp. cayenne pepper
- ½ tsp. ground cumin
- salt and black pepper

Directions:

1. Shred peeled potatoes and then drench in cold water. Stir the potatoes and let it soak until water is translucent – these are the starch from the potatoes. Drain water and then pour another batch of cold water. Repeat the Directions: again.
2. Transfer the potatoes in a flat tray and then pat dry using paper towels.
3. Preheat your Air Fryer to 390°F.
4. In a mixing bowl, combine together butter, cayenne pepper, cumin, salt, and black pepper. Add in the shredded potatoes and stir together.
5. Take out the Air Fryer cooking basket. Scoop about 2 Tbsp. of the potato mixture and then mold it to the desired shape. Place in the cooking basket.
6. Cook hash brown until golden brown for 15 minutes.
7. Serve and enjoy!

Nutritional Information:

Calories: 207
Fat: 9.3 g
Carbs: 30.1 g
Protein - 3.2 g

Breakfast Turkey Melt Sandwich

Servings: 4

Ingredients:

- 28g whole wheat bread, sliced
- 56g lean turkey ham, sliced
- 28g cheese slices
- 15g tomato, sliced
- butter, unsalted

Directions:

1. Each bread slice should be spread with 1 teaspoon butter on one side.
2. Top each buttered bread with cheese, turkey ham, and tomato slices. Cover with remaining bread slices.
3. Take two bread together and then place them together to make 4 sandwiches.
4. Preheat Air Fryer to 360°F.
5. Place sandwiches inside the Air Fryer cooking basket and then cook for 7-10 minutes or until bread turns golden brown.
6. Serve and enjoy!

Nutritional Information:

Calories: 294
Fat: 15g
Carbs: 25.3g
Protein: 16.8g

Deserving Cheesy Omelette

Servings: 1

Ingredients

- 2 eggs, beaten
- Pepper
- 1 c. shredded cheddar cheese
- 1 chopped onion
- 2 tbsps. soy sauce

Directions

1. Preheat your Air Fryer up to 340 degrees F.
2. Drizzle soy sauce over the chopped onions.
3. Place the onions in your air fryer's cooking basket and cook for 8 minutes.
4. In a medium bowl, mix the beaten eggs with salt and pepper.
5. Pour the egg mixture over onions (in the cooking basket) and cook for 3 minutes.
6. Add cheddar cheese over eggs and bake for 2 more minutes.
7. Serve with fresh basil and enjoy!

Nutritional Information:

Calories: 396
Fat: 32g
Carbs: 1g
Protein: 27g

Air Fried Cheese Soufflé

Servings: 6

Ingredients

- 1 oz. Panko breadcrumbs
- 2 oz. unsalted butter
- 56g all-purpose flour
- 1¼ c. skim milk
- 4 eggs
- ½ c. grated cheddar cheese
- ¼ c. grated parmesan cheese
- ½ tsp. nutmeg
- ½ tsp. vanilla extract
- powdered sugar
- olive oil spray

Directions:

1. Preheat your Air Fryer to 330°F.
2. Grease soufflé dishes with oil spray and sprinkle breadcrumbs.
3. In a small saucepan, melt butter and then add flour. Stir both ingredients together until you reach a smooth consistency. Transfer to a small bowl. Clean the saucepan for the next steps.
4. Heat milk and stir in vanilla extract in the cleaned saucepan. Bring to a boil. Add in the flour and butter mixture. Mix well until no lumps are visibly achieving a smooth consistency. Simmer the sauce until it thickens. Immediately transfer the saucepan over iced water for 10 minutes to cool.
5. In a mixing bowl, separate egg yolks from the egg whites.
6. Add the egg yolks to the thickened sauce. Stir in cheddar and parmesan. Season with nutmeg.
7. In another bowl, beat the egg whites until it reaches peak which can hold its shape. Then using a metal spoon, gradually stir in egg whites into the sauce mixture.
8. Divide mixture in soufflé dishes. Use a knife to even out the top of the soufflé dish.

9. Place soufflé dishes in Air Fryer cooking basket. Cook for about 15-18 minutes.
10. Sprinkle powdered sugar on cooked cheese soufflé.
11. Serve and enjoy!

Nutritional Information:

Calories: 238
Fat: 12g
Carbs: 15.3g
Protein: 11.9g

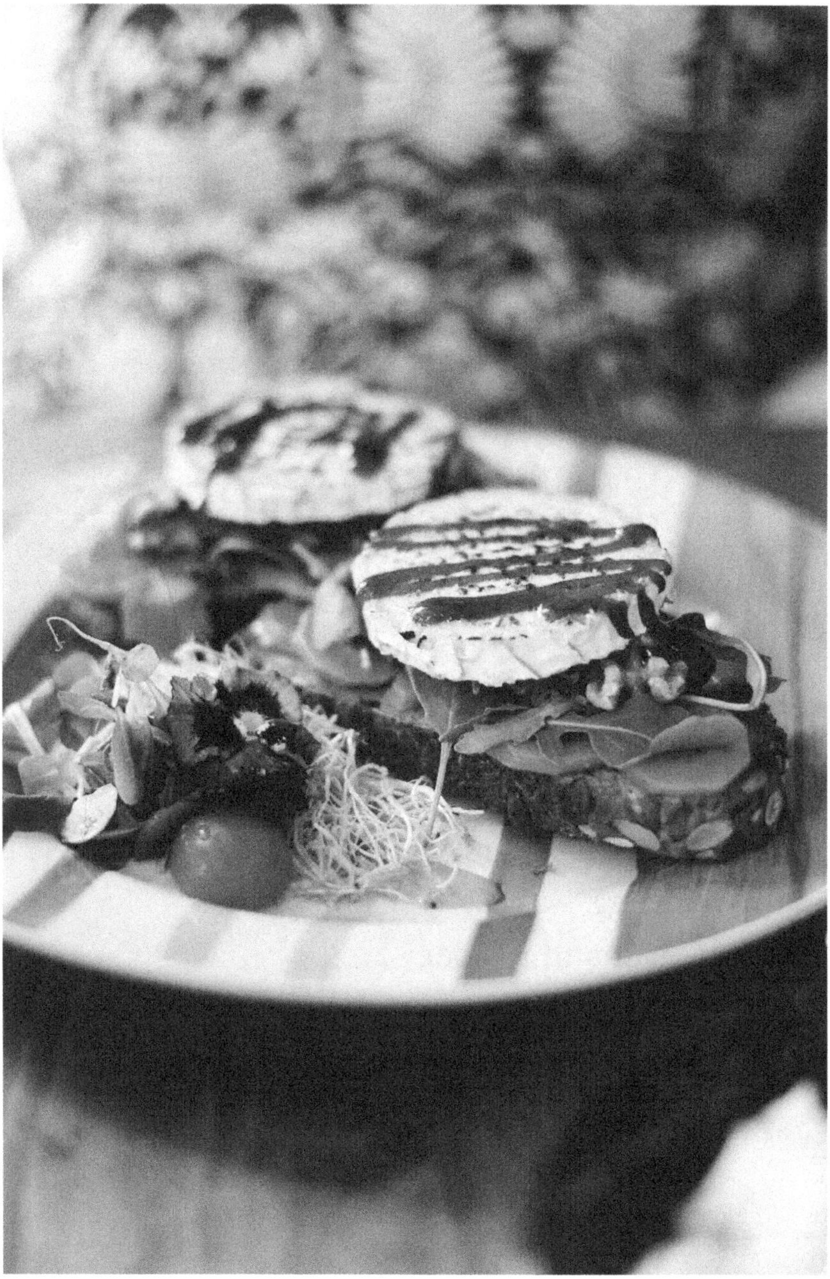

Chicken and Potato Nuggets

Servings: 4

Ingredients

- 1 lb. minced chicken breast fillet
- 1 c. mashed potato
- 1 egg
- salt and pepper
- olive oil spray

For the breading:

- 2 beaten eggs
- ¾ c. breadcrumbs
- salt and pepper

Directions:

1. Combine chicken, mashed potato, and egg in a mixing bowl. Season with salt and pepper to taste. Spoon about 1 ½ tablespoon of mixture and form into 1-inch thick bite-sized pieces (nuggets). Place in a large platter. Set aside as you prepare the breading ingredients.
2. In a mixing bowl, place breadcrumbs and season with salt and pepper.
3. Place seasoned breadcrumbs and eggs in separate bowls.
4. Coat each chicken and potato nugget with beaten eggs, and then in breadcrumbs.
5. Preheat your Air Fryer to 390°F.
6. Place chicken and potato nuggets in the cooking basket. Spray with oil. Do not overcrowd to have an equal distribution of heat while cooking.
7. Cook for about 7-10 minutes, or until golden brown.
8. Serve and enjoy!

Nutritional Information:

Calories: 271
Fat: 12.2g
Carbs: 16.1g
Protein: 24.2g

Herbed Cauliflower Quinoa and Cheese Casserole

Servings: 4

Ingredients

- 2 tbsps. unsalted butter
- 4 c. cauliflower florets
- 1 c. low-fat milk
- 2/3 c. cooked quinoa
- 2/3 c. cottage cheese crumbled
- ¼ c. parsley
- 4 oz. mozzarella cheese, grated
- sea salt
- Freshly ground black pepper

Directions:

1. Preheat your Air Fryer to 360°F.
2. In a saucepan, boil water. Add cauliflower florets and then cook for 1 minute. Drain and set aside.
3. In a mixing bowl, place cauliflower florets and then add butter, milk, quinoa, cottage cheese, and parsley. Season with salt and pepper to taste. Mix well together.
4. Transfer mixture into a casserole dish that can fit into the size of the Air Fryer cooking basket, cook in batches if needed. Sprinkle with mozzarella cheese.
5. Place casserole dish in Air Fryer cooking basket.
6. Cook for about 20-25 minutes, or until cooked through and cheese is melted.
7. Serve and enjoy!

Nutritional Information:

Calories: 239
Fat: 12.2g
Carbs: 16.1g
Protein: 16g

Home-made Sausage Frittata

Servings: 1

Ingredients

- ½ chopped sausage
- Salt and pepper
- Bunch of chopped parsley
- 3 whole eggs
- 1 tbsp. olive oil
- 1 slice bread
- 4 cherry tomatoes, chopped
- 1 slice bread
- 2 tbsps. shredded parmesan

Directions

1. Preheat your Air Fryer up to 360 degrees F.
2. Place tomatoes and sausages in your air fryer's cooking basket and bake for 5 minutes.
3. In a bowl, mix baked tomatoes, sausages, eggs, salt, parsley, parmesan, olive oil, and pepper.
4. Add the bread to the air fryer cooking basket and cook for 5 minutes.
5. Add the frittata mixture over baked bread and top with parmesan.
6. Serve and enjoy!

Nutritional Information:

Calories: 491
Fat: 33g
Carbs: 11g
Protein: 35g

Herbed Sweet Potato Hash

Servings: 5

Ingredients

- 4 sweet potatoes, peeled and diced
- 1 c. sliced button mushrooms
- 1 chopped onion
- ½ chopped green bell pepper
- 2 tbsps. lemon juice
- 2 tbsps. olive oil
- ½ tsp. thyme, dried
- ½ tsp. rosemary, dried
- salt, and pepper

Directions:

1. Preheat Air Fryer to 360°F.
2. In a mixing bowl, mix together all ingredients. Season with salt and pepper.
3. Take out Air Fryer cooking basket, and then place sweet potato mixture.
4. Cook for about 25-30 minutes.
5. Serve and enjoy!

Nutritional Information:

Calories: 203
Fat: 6.5g
Carbs: 36.2g
Protein: 3.4g

Spinach Frittata with Cherry Tomato and Cheddar

Servings: 4

Ingredients

- 6 eggs
- Kosher salt
- Ground black pepper
- 2 tbsps. olive oil
- 1 chopped onion
- 1 c. halved cherry tomatoes
- 8 oz. spinach leaves
- 3 oz. grated cheddar

Directions:

1. Preheat oven to 390°F.
2. In a mixing bowl, whisk 6 eggs together a season with salt and pepper to taste. Set aside.
3. Set a skillet over medium high heat and heat olive oil. Stir-fry the onion for 3 minutes, then add the spinach leaves and cherry tomatoes. Cook for 3 minutes stirring often.
4. Transfer vegetables in a small baking pan (enough to fit Air Fryer), pour the beaten eggs. Sprinkle with cheddar cheese.
5. Place baking pan in the Air Fryer cooking basket and cook for about 10 minutes.
6. Serve and enjoy!

Nutritional Information:

Calories: 215 calories
Fat: 12.9g
Carbs: 8.5g
Protein: 14.2g

Herbed Salmon and Cheese Frittata

Servings: 4

Ingredients

- 6 eggs
- Kosher salt
- Ground black pepper
- 2 tbsps. olive oil
- 1 chopped white onion
- 1 minced clove garlic
- 8 oz. baked salmon, diced
- 2 tbsps. freshly chopped dill weed
- 2 oz. grated cheddar
- 2 tbsps. chopped parsley

Directions:

1. Preheat oven to 390°F.
2. In a mixing bowl, whisk 6 eggs together and season with salt and pepper to taste.
3. Heat olive oil in a skillet over medium heat. Stir-fry onion and garlic for 3 minutes. Add the salmon and dill; cook further 2-3 minutes.
4. Transfer mixture in a small baking dish (enough to fit the Air Fryer cooking basket), pour the beaten egg mixture. Sprinkle with cheddar cheese.
5. Place baking dish in the Air Fryer cooking basket and cook for about 10 minutes.
6. Transfer into a baking dish and sprinkle with chopped parsley.
7. Serve and enjoy!

Nutritional Information:

Calories: 217
Fat: 12.5g
Carbs: 4.7g
Protein: 18.8g

Asparagus & Bacon Spears

Servings: 4

Ingredients:

- 20 spears asparagus
- 4 bacon slices
- 1 tbsp. olive oil
- 1 tbsp. sesame oil
- 1 crushed garlic clove

Directions:

1. Pre-heat your Air Fryer to 380 degrees F
2. Take a small bowl and add oil, crushed garlic, and mix
3. Separate asparagus into 4 bunches and wrap them in bacon
4. Brush wraps with oil and garlic mix, transfer to your Air Fryer basket
5. Cook for 8 minutes
6. Serve and enjoy!

Nutritional Information:

Calories: 175
Fat: 15g
Carbs: 6
Protein: 5g

Tender Potato Pancakes

Servings: 4

Ingredients:

- 4 potatoes, peeled and cleaned
- 1 chopped onion
- 1 beaten egg
- ¼ c. milk
- 2 tbsps. unsalted butter
- ½ tsp. garlic powder
- ¼ tsp. salt
- 3 tbsps. all-purpose flour
- Pepper

Directions:

1. Peel your potatoes and shred them up.
2. Soak the shredded potatoes under cold water to remove starch.
3. Drain the potatoes.
4. Take a bowl and add eggs, milk, butter, garlic powder, salt, and pepper.
5. Add in flour.
6. Mix well.
7. Add the shredded potatoes.
8. Pre-heat your air fryer to 390 degrees F.
9. Add ¼ cup of the potato pancake batter to your cooking basket and cook for 12 minutes until the golden brown texture is seen.
10. Enjoy!

Nutritional Information:

Calories: 248
Fat: 11g
Carbs: 33g
Protein: 6g

Bacon Egg Muffins

Servings: 2

Ingredients:

- 1 whole egg
- 2 streaky bacon
- 1 English muffin
- Salt and pepper

Directions:

1. Pre-heat your Air Fryer to 200 degrees F.
2. Take an oven proof bowl and crack in the egg.
3. Take Air Fryer cooking basket and add bacon, egg, and muffin into Fryer.
4. Cook for 7 minutes.
5. Assemble muffin done by packing bacon and egg on top of English muffin.
6. Serve and enjoy!

Nutritional Information:

Calories: 683
Fat: 48g
Carbs: 38g
Protein: 24g

Air Fryer Baked Cheesy Eggs

Servings: 2

Ingredients:

- 2 eggs
- 2 tbsps. milk
- 1 tsp. parmesan cheese
- 1 chopped tomato
- Salt and pepper
- 1 bacon slice
- Parsley, chopped

Directions:

1. Pre-heat your oven to 180 degrees F.
2. Over medium heat, set on a skillet and cook bacon (with a little bit of oil).
3. Cut bacon into small pieces and divide them equally amongst two ramekins.
4. Dice tomatoes and add them to the ramekins.
5. Add a tablespoon of milk onto each ramekin.
6. Crack an egg into each ramekin.
7. Season both with salt and pepper.
8. Sprinkle ½ teaspoon parmesan into ramekins.
9. Place ramekins into Air Fryer cooking basket and cook for 7 minutes.
10. Serve with a garnish of parsley and enjoy!

Nutritional Information:

Calories: 179
Fat: 11g
Carbs: 13g
Protein: 8g

Air Fried Mac & Cheese

Servings: 2

Ingredients:

- 1 c. elbow macaroni
- ½ c. broccoli
- ½ c. warm milk
- 1½ cheddar cheese, grated
- Salt and pepper
- 1 tbsp. parmesan cheese, grated

Directions:

1. Pre-heat your Fryer to 400 degrees F.
2. Take a pot and add water, allow it to boil.
3. Add macaroni and broccoli and broil for about 10 minutes until the mixture is Al Dente.
4. Drain the pasta and vegetables.
5. Toss the Past and veggies with cheese.
6. Season with some pepper and salt and transfer the mixture to your Fryer.
7. Sprinkle some more parmesan on top and cook for about 15 minutes.
8. Allow it to cool for about 10 minutes once done.
9. Enjoy!

Nutritional Information:

Calories: 183
Fat: 11g
Carbs: 14g
Protein: 6g

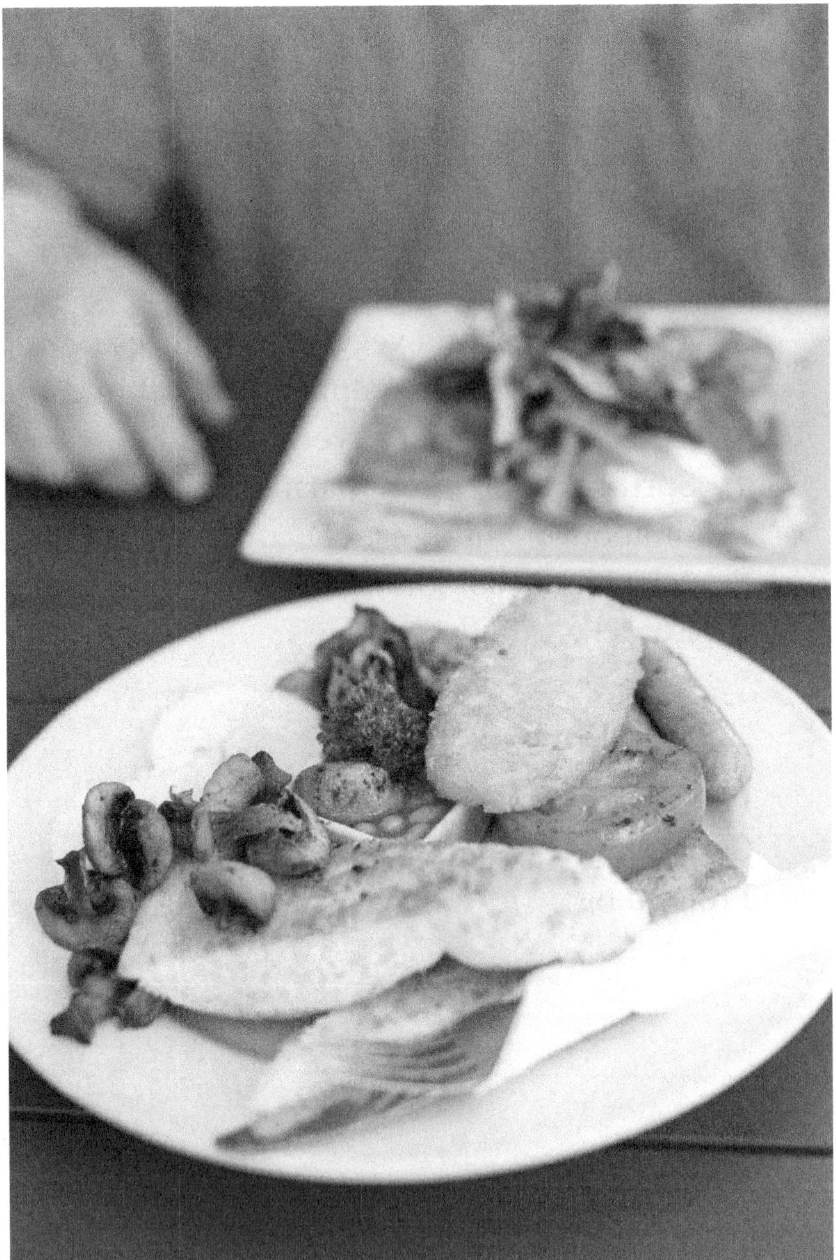

Main Dish

Roasted Salmon with Lemon and Rosemary

Servings: 4

Ingredients

- 4 salmon steak
- 2 tbsps. unsalted butter
- 2 tbsps. lemon juice
- 1 tsp. garlic, minced
- 2 tbsps. freshly chopped rosemary
- Himalayan salt
- freshly ground black pepper

Directions:

1. In a dish mix garlic, butter, rosemary, and lemon juice; add the salmon steaks and rub with a mixture. Cover and let it sit inside the refrigerator for 30 minutes.
2. Preheat your Air Fryer to 390°F.
3. Place the marinated salmon steaks in cooking basket and cook for about 8-10 minutes.
4. Transfer into a serving dish. Garnish with fresh rosemary leaves.
5. Serve and enjoy!

Nutritional Information:

Calories: 209
Fat: 12.1 g
Carbs: 2.3 g
Protein: 22.4 g

Air Fried Meatballs with Parsley

Servings: 5

Ingredients

- 1 chopped onion
- 1 tsp. minced garlic
- 1 lb. lean ground beef
- ¼ c. chopped parsley leaves
- ½ tsp. ground coriander seeds
- ¼ tsp. ground fennel seeds
- 1 egg
- 2 tsps. Worcestershire sauce
- ½ c. breadcrumbs
- sea salt
- ground black pepper

Directions:

1. In a mixing bowl, mix all ingredients.
2. Take about 2 tablespoons of beef mixture and form into small balls.
3. Preheat your Air Fryer to 390°F.
4. Place meatballs in the Air Fryer basket and cook until browned for 10 minutes.
5. Set into a serving bowl and spread with parsley.
6. Enjoy!

Nutritional Information:

Calories: 233
Fat: 7.2g
Carbs: 10.3g
Protein: 30.3g

Succulent Flank Steak

Servings: 4

Ingredients

- 4 flank steak
- ¼ c. olive oil
- ¼ c. red wine vinegar
- 1 tbsp. light soy sauce
- 1 Tbsp. Worcestershire sauce
- 1 Tbsp. Dijon mustard
- 1 tsp. garlic, minced
- Salt and ground black pepper

Directions:

1. In a non-reactive bowl, combine together olive oil, red wine vinegar, light soy sauce, Worcestershire sauce, Dijon mustard, and garlic. Add the steaks and mix to coat well. Cover and let it sit for 30 minutes inside the refrigerator.
2. Preheat Air Fryer to 360°F.
3. Place marinated steaks inside the Air Fryer cooking basket and cook for about 6-7 minutes (medium-rare) or 8-10 minutes (well-done).
4. Transfer into a serving dish.
5. Serve and enjoy!

Nutritional Information:

Calories: 280
Fat: 14.2g
Carbs: 1.5g
Protein: 34.1 g

Chili Roasted Eggplant Soba

Servings: 4 servings

Ingredients

- 200g eggplants
- Kosher salt
- Ground black pepper

Noodles:

- 8 oz. soba noodles
- 1 c. sliced button mushrooms
- 2 tbsps. peanut oil
- 2 tbsps. light soy sauce
- 1 Tbsp. rice vinegar
- 2 tbsps. chopped cilantro
- 2 chopped red chili pepper
- 1 tsp. sesame oil

Directions:

1. In a mixing bowl, mix together ingredients for the marinade.
2. Wash eggplants and then slice into ¼-inch thick cuts. Season with salt and pepper, to taste.
3. Preheat your Air Fryer to 390°F.
4. Place eggplants in the Air Fryer cooking basket. Cook for 10 minutes.
5. Meanwhile, cook the soba noodles according to packaging directions. Drain the noodles.
6. In a large mixing bowl, combine the peanut oil, soy sauce, rice vinegar, cilantro, chili, and sesame oil. Mix well.
7. Add the cooked soba noodles, mushrooms, and roasted eggplants; toss to coat.
8. Transfer mixture into the Air Fryer cooking basket. Cook for another 5 minutes.
9. Serve and enjoy!

Nutritional Information:

Calories: 318
Fat: 8.2g
Carbs: 54g
Protein: 11.3g

Quinoa and Spinach Cakes

Servings: 10

Ingredients

- 2 c. cooked quinoa
- 1 c. chopped baby spinach
- 1 egg
- 2 tbsps. minced parsley
- 1 tsp. minced garlic
- 1 carrot, peeled and shredded
- 1 chopped onion
- ¼ c. skim milk
- ¼ c. parmesan cheese, grated
- 1 c. breadcrumbs
- sea salt
- Ground black pepper

Directions:

1. In a mixing bowl, mix all ingredients. Season with salt and pepper to taste.
2. Preheat your Air Fryer to 390°F.
3. Scoop ¼ cup of quinoa and spinach mixture and place in the Air Fryer cooking basket. Cook in batches until browned for about 8 minutes.
4. Serve and enjoy!

Nutritional Information:

Calories: 188
Fat: 4.4 g
Carbs: 31.2g
Protein: 8.1g

Air Fried Cajun Shrimp

Servings: 5

Ingredients

- 1 lb. fresh shrimp
- 2 tbsps. olive oil
- 1 tsp. Spanish paprika
- ½ tsp. garlic powder
- ½ tsp. ground cumin
- ¼ tsp. oregano
- ¼ tsp. thyme
- ¼ tsp. ground black pepper
- ¼ tsp. sea salt

Directions:

1. In a bowl, mix all spice ingredients.
2. Add the shrimps and drizzle with olive oil. Toss to coat well. Cover and place inside the refrigerator to 30 minutes.
3. Preheat your Air Fryer to 390°F.
4. Transfer the shrimps into your Air Fryer cooking basket and cook for about 5-7 minutes.
5. Serve immediately and enjoy!

Nutritional Information:

Calories: 156
Fat: 7.2 g
Carbs: 3.8 g
Protein: 22.3 g

Air Fried Squid Rings

Servings: 5

Ingredients

- 1 lb. frozen squid/calamari rings, thawed, washed, and dried
- 1 egg, beaten
- 1 c. all-purpose flour
- 1 tsp. ground coriander seeds
- 1 tsp. cayenne pepper
- ½ tsp. ground black pepper
- ½ tsp. kosher salt
- Lemon wedges
- olive oil spray

Directions:

1. In a mixing bowl, combine all-purpose flour, paprika, cayenne pepper, salt and ground pepper.
2. Coat each calamari ring with egg and then flour mixture.
3. Preheat Air Fryer to 390°F.
4. Place coated calamari rings in the Air Fryer cooking basket. Spray with oil. Cook until browned for about 10 minutes. Cook in batches if needed.
5. Add lemon wedges for garnish and serve alongside tartar sauce.
6. Enjoy!

Nutritional Information:

Calories: 238
Fat: 8.9g
Carbs: 22.7g
Protein: 18.4g

Marinated Portabello Mushroom

Servings: 4

Ingredients

- 4 pcs. portabello mushrooms
- 1 chopped shallot
- 1 tsp. minced garlic
- 2 tbsps. olive oil
- 2 tbsps. balsamic vinegar
- Sea salt
- Ground black pepper

Directions:

1. Clean and wash portabello mushrooms and remove stems. Set aside.
2. In a bowl, mix together the shallot, garlic, olive oil, and balsamic vinegar. Season with salt and pepper, to taste.
3. Arrange portabello mushrooms, cap side up and brush with balsamic vinegar mixture. Let it stand for at least 30 minutes.
4. Preheat your Air Fryer to 360°F.
5. Place marinated portabello mushroom on Air Fryer cooking basket. Cook for about 15-20 minutes or until mushrooms are tender.
6. Serve and enjoy!

Nutritional Information:

Calories: 96
Fat: 7.9g
Carbs: 7.5g
Protein: 3.6g

Air Fried Meatloaf

Servings: 6

Ingredients

- 1½ lbs. lean ground beef
- 2 tbsps. chopped onion
- 1 egg
- ¾ c. breadcrumbs
- ¼ c. skim milk
- 1 tbsp. chopped fresh oregano
- 1 tbsp. chopped basil
- 1 tsp. brown sugar
- 2 tbsps. Dijon mustard
- 1/3 c. tomato sauce
- Sea salt
- Ground black pepper

Directions:

1. In a mixing bowl, mix ground beef and the rest of the meatloaf ingredients. Mix well with your hands until incorporated well. Season with salt and pepper to taste.
2. Preheat your Air Fryer to 330°F.
3. Place meatloaf in a baking dish or loaf pan that can fit into your Air Fryer basket. Then, place inside the Air Fryer and cook for 30 minutes. Cool slightly.
4. Serve and enjoy!

Nutritional Information:

Calories: 269
Fat: 8.3g
Carbs: 10.8g
Protein: 35.7g

Fettuccini with Roasted Vegetables in Tomato Sauce

Servings: 4

Ingredients

- 10 oz. dry fettuccine, cooked
- 1 eggplant, chopped
- 1 chopped bell pepper
- 1 zucchini, chopped
- 4 oz. halved grape tomatoes
- 1 tsp. minced garlic
- 4 tbsps. divided olive oil
- Kosher salt
- Ground black pepper
- 12 oz. can diced tomatoes
- ½ tsp. dried basil
- ½ tsp. dried oregano
- 1 tsp. Spanish paprika
- 1 tsp. brown sugar

Directions:

1. In a mixing bowl, combine together eggplant, red bell pepper, zucchini, grape tomatoes, garlic, and 2 tablespoons olive oil. Add some salt and pepper, to taste.
2. Preheat your Air Fryer to 390°F.
3. Place vegetable mixture in the Air Fryer cooking basket and cook for about 10-12 minutes, or until vegetables are tender.
4. Meanwhile, you can start preparing the tomato sauce.
5. In a saucepan, heat remaining 2 tablespoons olive oil. Stir fry garlic for 2 minutes. Add diced tomatoes and simmer for 3 minutes.
6. Stir in basil, oregano, paprika, and brown sugar. Season with salt and pepper, to taste. Let it cook for another 5-7 minutes.
7. Once cooked, transfer the vegetables from Air Fryer to a mixing bowl.
8. Add the cooked pasta and prepared a sauce. Toss to combine well.
9. Divide among 4 serving plates.
10. Serve and enjoy!

Nutritional Information:

Calories: 330
Fat: 12.4g
Carbs: 45.3g
Protein: 9.9g

Herbed Parmesan Turkey Meatballs

Servings: 5

Ingredients

- 1 chopped onion
- 1 tsp. minced garlic
- 1 lb. lean ground turkey breast
- 1 Tbsp. chopped parsley leaves
- 1 Tbsp. chopped rosemary
- 1 egg
- ½ c. breadcrumbs
- ¼ c. grated parmesan cheese
- Kosher salt
- Pepper
- cooking oil spray

Directions:

1. In a mixing bowl, combine ingredients together. Mix well.
2. Take about 2 tablespoons of beef mixture and form into small balls.
3. Preheat Air Fryer to 390°F.
4. Place meatballs in the Air Fryer cooking basket. Spray with oil and cook until browned for 15 minutes.
5. Transfer into a serving dish. Sprinkle with parmesan cheese and more chopped parsley, if desired.
6. Serve turkey meatballs as is or with your choice of sauce.
7. Enjoy!

Nutritional Information:

Calories: 214
Fat: 9.4g
Carbs: 13.2g
Protein: 19.1g

Teriyaki Glazed Salmon and Vegetable Roast

Servings: 4

Ingredients

- 4 salmon fillets
- 2 diced tomatoes
- 1 red bell pepper, deseeded and chopped
- 1 yellow red bell pepper, deseeded and chopped
- 1 sliced zucchini
- cooking oil spray
- Kosher salt
- Ground black pepper

For the marinade:

- ¼ c. mirin (Japanese cooking wine)
- ¼ c. orange juice
- 2 tbsps. olive oil
- 2 tbsps. soy sauce, low-sodium
- 1 Tbsp. lemon juice
- 1 Tbsp. honey
- 1 tsp. ground ginger
- 1 tsp. minced garlic

Directions:

1. Combine marinade ingredients in a mixing bowl. Mix well. Divide among two shallow bowls.
2. Add the salmon fillets in one bowl with marinade and the vegetables in another bowl. Toss to coat well. Cover with plastic wrap and let sit in the refrigerator for 30 minutes.
3. Preheat your Air Fryer to 360°F.
4. Transfer the marinated salmon and place into the Air Fryer cooking basket along with the marinated vegetables. Cook for 8-10 minutes.
5. Serve and enjoy.

Nutritional Information:

Calories: 290
Fat: 12.4g
Carbs: 16.3g
Protein: 24.2g

Sirloin with Garlic and Thyme

Servings: 4

Ingredients

- 4 (5 oz. each) sirloin steak

Steak Rub:

- 2 tbsps. low-sodium steak sauce
- 2 tbsps. olive oil
- 1 Tbsp. freshly chopped thyme
- 1 tsp. minced garlic
- ½ tsp. ground coriander seeds
- ¼ tsp. kosher salt
- ¼ tsp. freshly ground black pepper

Directions:

1. Preheat Air Fryer to 360°F.
2. Mix together all steak rub ingredients in a mixing bowl. Add the steak and rub with this mixture. Cover and let sit for 30 minutes inside the refrigerator.
3. Place steaks in the Air Fryer cooking basket. Cook for 8-10 minutes (medium rare) or 12-15 minutes (well-done).
4. Serve and enjoy!

Nutritional Information:

Calories: 274
Fat: 12.2g
Carbs: 0.7g
Protein: 34.5 g

Air Fried Chicken Tenders with Honey Mustard Dip

Servings: 6

Ingredients

- 1 lb. chicken tenders
For the Breading:
- ¾ c. all-purpose flour
- ½ tsp. Kosher salt
- ¼ tsp. black pepper
- 2 beaten eggs
- ¾ c. seasoned breadcrumbs
- cooking oil spray

For the Honey Mustard Dip:
- ½ c. low-fat mayonnaise
- 2 tbsps. Dijon mustard
- 1½ tbsps. pure honey
- 2 tsps. lemon juice

Directions:

1. In a mixing bowl, season all-purpose flour with salt and pepper.
2. Place eggs and breadcrumbs in separate bowls.
3. Coat chicken tenders first with seasoned flour, then eggs and lastly, breadcrumbs.
4. Preheat Air Fryer to 390°F.
5. Place breaded chicken tenders in Air Fryer cooking basket. Spray lightly with oil. Cook until golden brown for 10 minutes.
6. As the chicken tenders are being cooked, prepare the Honey-Mustard Dip.
7. In a mixing bowl, whisk all dip ingredients. Transfer in a small bowl and then cover. Refrigerate until ready to serve.
8. Transfer the chicken tenders into a serving dish and serve with Honey-Mustard dip on the side.
9. Serve and enjoy.

Nutritional Information:

Calories: 244
Fat: 10g
Carbs: 17.9g
Protein: 20g

Fish and Lentil Burger Patties

Servings: 4 (2 patties each)

Ingredients

- 10 oz. cream dory fillets, steamed and flaked
- 1 c. cooked lentils
- 1 beaten egg
- 1 chopped onion
- 1 red bell pepper, deseeded and chopped
- 1 chopped celery stalk
- 2/3 c. breadcrumbs
- 2 tbsps. chopped cilantro
- 1 tsp. dried thyme
- ½ tsp. garlic powder
- Kosher salt
- Ground black pepper

Directions:

1. In a plate, place cooked dory fillets and use a fork to flake the fish.
2. In a mixing bowl, mix the flaked dory with the rest of the ingredients. Season with salt and pepper. Mix well.
3. Scoop about ¼ cup of mixture and form into patties.
4. Preheat Air Fryer to 390°F.
5. Place fish 2-3 patties in the Air Fryer cooking basket. Cook until golden brown for approximately 10 minutes. Repeat with remaining patties.
6. Serve with a fresh salad on the side.
7. Enjoy!

Nutritional Information:

Calories: 276
Fat: 10.1g
Carbs: 23.4g
Protein: 22.7g

Korean Style Chicken Thighs

Servings: 8

Ingredients:

- 3 tbsps. honey
- ½ c. soy sauce
- ¼ tsp. ground ginger
- 3 tbsps. sesame oil
- 8 chicken thighs
- ¼ tsp. black pepper
- 2 tsps. minced garlic
- ½ c. chopped green onion

Directions:

1. In a bowl, combine the honey, sesame oil, soy sauce, sliced onions, ginger, and garlic. Stir in the black pepper.
2. Preheat your air fryer to 400 °F. Arrange the chicken thighs in an air fryer basket, lined with foil.
3. Spoon the mixture over, set the timer for 14 minutes and cook turning over 1-2 times through the cooking time.

Nutritional Information:

Calories: 296
Fat: 13.5g
Carbs: 8.5g
Protein: 34g

Almond Crusted Chicken Fingers

Servings: 4

Ingredients:

- 1 lb. chicken breast
- ½ c. almond meal
- 1 beaten egg
- ½ tsp. salt
- ¾ tsp. Paprika
- ¼ tsp. ground coriander seeds
- ¼ tsp. ground cumin seeds

Directions:

1. Preheat the air fryer to 400 °F. In a shallow dish mix the almond meal, coriander, and cumin seeds, salt, and pepper.
2. In a small bowl, lightly beat the egg. Coat the chicken pieces with egg, and then roll in the almond meal mixture until evenly coated.
3. Place the chicken strips in the basket of your air fryer lined with parchment and cook for 15 minutes, until golden brown.
4. If you want your chicken strips to be evenly brown, turn them 1-2 times through the cooking time.

Nutritional Information:

Calories: 127
Fat: 8.7g
Carbs: 2.9g
Protein: 10.2g

Roast Pork Loin with Red Potatoes

Servings: 4

Ingredients:

- 2 lbs. pork loin
- 2 red potatoes, cut
- 1 tsp. salt
- 1 tsp. pepper
- ½ tsp. garlic powder
- ½ tsp. red pepper flakes
- 1 tsp. parsley

Directions:

1. Place the potatoes and pork in a bowl and season with garlic powder, red pepper flakes, salt, and pepper.
2. Place the pork in the basket of the air fryer, place the potatoes around and cook at 360° F for 25 minutes.
3. Remove the pork from the air fryer, and let it sit for 10 minutes.
4. Place the fried potatoes in a serving dish. Cut the pork into thin slices and place on top
5. Garnish with chopped parsley and serve warm.

Nutritional Information:

Calories: 627
Fat: 31.8g
Carbs: 17.7g
Protein: 64.1g

Beef Zucchini Patties with Feta Cheese

Servings: 4

Ingredients:

- 1½ lbs. ground beef
- ½ c. sour cream
- 1 ½ c. grated zucchini
- ½ tsp. ground cinnamon
- 2 tsps. ground cumin
- 5 oz. divided feta cheese
- 2 tbsps. fresh lemon juice
- ½ tsp. salt
- ½ tsp. pepper

Directions:

1. In a bowl, add zucchini and ground beef. Season with salt, pepper, cumin, and cinnamon and mix well to combine.
2. Shape the mixture into 10-12 patties.
3. Preheat your air fryer to 400 °F.
4. Line the basket with parchment and lightly coat with oil. Place the patties in the basket and cook for 20 minutes flipping halfway through the cooking time.
5. In a small bowl, mix the feta, sour cream, and lemon juice.
6. Place the browned patties on a serving plate and top each of them with 3 tablespoons of the prepared feta sauce.
7. Enjoy.

Nutritional Information:

Calories: 349
Fat: 19g
Carbs: 3.5g
Protein: 34g

Portobello Pizza

Servings: 3

Ingredients:

- 3 Portobello mushrooms
- 3 tsps. Pizza Seasoning
- Olive Oil
- 3 slices tomato
- 1.5 oz. mozzarella cheese
- 1.5 oz. Monterey Jack
- 12 Pepperoni slices
- 1.5 oz. Cheddar cheese

Directions:

1. Preheat the air fryer to 400 °F.
2. Rinse the mushrooms and remove the stems.
3. Arrange the mushrooms in the basket of your air fryer cap side down. Drizzle with little olive oil.
4. Sprinkle with pizza seasoning
5. Top with a slice of tomato, followed by the mix of grated cheese and again sprinkle with pizza seasoning.
6. Bake in the air fryer for 6 minutes until the cheese melts.
7. Finally, top the mushrooms with pepperoni and cook for another 2 minutes.
8. Remove from the air fryer and enjoy.

Nutritional Information:

Calories: 227
Fat: 17.1g
Carbs: 45g
Protein: 15.3g

Bacon Wrapped Chicken

Servings: 2

Ingredients:

- 2 chicken breasts, cut
- 4 slices bacon
- 4 oz. cheddar cheese
- Salt and Pepper

Directions:

1. Apply pepper and salt to the chicken fillets. Then sprinkle with grated cheese.
2. Wrap the bacon tightly over the chicken breasts and secure with a toothpick.
3. Arrange in the air fryer basket coated with cooking spray and cook in the air fryer at 320 °F for 17 minutes, until the chicken is cooked through.

Nutritional Information:

Calories: 590
Fat: 30g
Carbs: 32.4g
Protein: 57.9g

Air fried Fish Cakes

Servings: 2

Ingredients:

- 2 cod fish filets
- ½ c. flour
- 3 eggs
- 1 tsp. light soy sauce
- 2 cloves garlic
- 3 chopped green onions
- 2 small chilies
- Salt and pepper

Directions:

1. In a shallow bowl, beat the eggs.
2. Thinly chop the onions, garlic, and chilies and add to the eggs. Mix well.
3. Remove the skin of the fish and cut into medium size cubes. Dip your fish cakes in the egg mixture, and then coat them with flour.
4. Air-fry, the fish pieces at 380 °F for 7 minutes, turning over once through the cooking time.

Nutritional Information:

Calories: 369
Fat: 8.1g
Carbs: 27g
Protein: 44.5g

Turkey Meatballs

Servings: 4-6

Ingredients:

- 2 lbs. lean ground turkey
- 1½ tsps. salt
- 1 tsp. dried sage leaves
- ½ tsp. ground ginger
- 1 tsp. pepper
- ½ tsp. cayenne pepper

Directions:

1. In a bowl, set the ground turkey. Add the cayenne pepper, ginger, salt, pepper, and sage, and mix well to combine.
2. Preheat the air fryer to 360°F. Arrange the meatballs in the basket of your air fryer and set the timer to 15 minutes.
3. Using a spatula, turn them over halfway through the cooking time so that they are evenly browned on all sides.
4. Enjoy with your favorite vegetable salad.

Nutritional Information:

Calories: 327
Fat: 16.3g
Carbs: 0.7g
Protein: 44.7g

Air Fryer Baked Garlic Parsley Potatoes

Servings: 4

Ingredients:

- 3 russet potatoes
- 2 tbsps. olive oil
- 1 tbsp. salt
- 1 tbsp. garlic powder
- 1 tsp. parsley

Directions:

1. Rinse the potatoes under running water and pierce with a fork in several places.
2. Season with salt and garlic and drizzle with olive oil. Rub the seasonings with your hands, so the potatoes are evenly coated.
3. Put the potatoes in the basket of your air fryer and slide it into the air fryer.
4. Set the temperature of 400 °F and the timer for 35 minutes and turn the button On Check the doneness and once the potatoes are fork tender remove from the fryer.
5. Serve the potatoes garnished with chopped fresh parsley and topped with a dollop of sour cream.

Nutritional Information:

Calories: 147
Fat: 3.7g
Carbs: 26.7g
Protein: 3g

Roasted Chicken Breast and Vegetables

Servings: 4

Ingredients

- 4 chicken breasts
- 1 tbsp. Dijon mustard
- 1 tbsp. honey
- ½ tsp. garlic powder
- ½ tsp. dried rosemary
- ½ tsp. cayenne pepper
- 2 tbsps. olive oil
- 2 tbsps. lemon juice
- 1 tsp. minced garlic
- ½ tsp. dried basil
- 2 c. broccoli florets
- 2 sliced carrot
- 1 lb. marbled potatoes washed thoroughly
- salt and pepper

Directions:

1. Preheat your Air Fryer to 360°F.
2. In a shallow dish, place the chicken breast. Add the mustard, honey, garlic powder, rosemary, and cayenne pepper. Mix to coat well.
3. In a bowl, combine the olive oil, lemon juice, garlic, and basil. Add the vegetables and toss to coat. Season with salt and pepper.
4. Place the vegetables in the Air Fryer cooking basket and cook for 20-25 minutes, or until potatoes are tender. Transfer vegetables to a plate and tent with foil to keep warm.
5. Place the marinated chicken breasts inside the same Air Fryer cooking basket and cook for about 20 minutes or until cooked through.
6. Serve chicken with roasted vegetables on the side.
7. Enjoy!

Nutritional Information:

Calories: 276
Fat: 12.2g
Carbs: 17.4 g
Protein: 25.1g

Roasted Green Beans with Shrimp

Servings: 4

Ingredients:

Green beans:
- 1 lb. green beans, trimmed, cut
- 1½ tbsps. olive oil
- ½ tsp. ground coriander
- ½ tsp. ground cumin
- ½ tsp. salt
- ½ tsp. fresh ground black pepper
- 1/8 tsp. cayenne pepper

Shrimp:
- ¾ lb. raw shrimp, peeled
- 1½ tbsps. olive oil
- Zest of 1 lemon
- ½ tsp. salt
- ½ tsp. ground black pepper

Directions:

1. Preheat the air fryer to 360 °F. Trim your green beans, cut and place in a medium bowl. Add ground coriander, olive oil, ground cumin, salt, and black and cayenne peppers. Toss well to coat.
2. In a separate bowl, combine the peeled shrimp with olive oil, lemon zest, salt, and freshly ground black pepper.
3. Coat the air fryer basket with olive oil and spread the beans in it.
4. Cook for 8 minutes is shaking the basket 1-2 times through the cooking time.
5. Then top the beans with shelled shrimp and continue cooking for another 10 minutes.
6. Transfer to a serving dish, drizzle with freshly squeezed lemon juice and serve immediately.

Nutritional Information:

Calories: 229
Fat: 12.2g
Carbs: 9.9g
Protein: 21.6g

Air-fried Chicken Skewers

Servings: 4-6

Ingredients:

- ¼ c. olive oil
- 2 tsps. red wine vinegar
- 2 tbsps. chopped oregano
- 1 tbsp. shallot or red onion, minced
- 1 tsp. minced garlic
- ¼ tsp. red pepper flakes
- 1 head romaine lettuce, quartered
- 1½ lbs. skinless, boneless chicken breasts or thighs
- 1½ c. breadcrumbs

Directions:

1. Preheat your air fryer to 360 °F.
2. Mix the garlic, olive oil, oregano, vinegar, red pepper flakes, shallot, and 1 1/4 teaspoons salt in a large bowl.
3. Reserve 2-3 teaspoons of mixture.
4. Add in the chicken and toss well with your hands. Let it sit for 15 minutes. Sprinkle the chicken with breadcrumbs and toss to coat.
5. Then thread the chicken pieces onto the wooden skewers and place in the basket of the air fryer.
6. Set the timer for 15 minutes and cook the chicken skewers, turning 1-2 times through the cooking time, until they acquire golden crust.
7. Enjoy.

Nutritional Information:

Calories: 523
Fat: 23g
Carbs: 31g
Protein 43g

Rosemary Lamb Chops

Servings: 6

Ingredients:

- 1 tbsp. chopped rosemary
- 1 tsp. olive oil
- ½ tsp. kosher salt, divided
- 1 garlic clove, minced
- 4 lamb loin chops, trimmed
- 1/8 tsp. ground black pepper
- Cooking spray

Directions:

1. In a bowl, mix the rosemary, oil, garlic, and 1/4 teaspoon salt.
2. Coat the lamb chops with marinade mixture and let them sit in the refrigerator for 2-3 hours.
3. When ready to cook, preheat the air fryer to 360 °F. Lightly oil the basket of your air fryer.
4. Remove the lamb from the fridge and season the chops with the remaining 1/4 teaspoon salt and pepper and place in the basket.
5. Set the timer for 15 minutes and let them cook flipping over once through the cooking time.
6. Remove from the fryer and serve warm.

Nutritional Information:

Calories: 232
Fat: 15.2g
Carbs: 0.5g
Protein: 22g

Grilled Steak with Red Onion and Tomatoes

Servings: 4

Ingredients:

- 2 lbs. flank steak, fat trimmed
- 2 tbsps. balsamic
- 1/3 c. chopped red onion
- Garlic powder
- 3-4 chopped tomatoes
- 1 tbsp. basil or parsley
- 1 tbsp. olive oil
- Kosher salt
- Fresh pepper

Directions:

1. Rub pepper, salt and garlic powder to the steak. Set aside at room temperature for 15 minutes.
2. In a bowl, mix balsamic, olive oil, pepper, onions and salt. Set aside for 5 minutes.
3. Then stir in the chopped tomatoes and herbs. Preheat your air fryer to 400 °F for 5 minutes.
4. Place the steak in a small baking pan that fits into the air fryer basket and slides the basket into the air fryer.
5. Set the timer for 8 minutes for medium rare or cook longer to reach to your desired doneness.
6. Set on a serving plate and allow to cool before slicing.
7. Slice the steak, apply a topping of tomato mixture and enjoy.

Nutritional Information:

Calories: 487
Fat: 22.5g
Carbs: 3.7g
Protein: 63.9g

Chicken Bruschetta

Servings: 4

Ingredients:

- 3 ripe tomatoes, cubed
- 2 minced cloves garlic
- ¼ c. chopped red onion
- 2 tbsps. chopped basil leaves
- 1 tbsp. balsamic vinegar
- 3 oz. diced mozzarella
- 8 thinly sliced chicken cutlets
- 1 tbsp. olive oil
- Salt and ground black pepper

Directions:

1. Place cubed tomatoes in a bowl. Mix in balsamic, pepper, onion, basil olive oil and garlic. Set aside for 15-20 minutes to blend the flavors. Mix in the cheese when ready to serve.
2. Preheat your air fryer to 360 °F.
3. Apply black pepper and salt to the chicken.
4. Coat the air fryer basket with cooking spray.
5. Place the chicken cutlets in the basket and cook for 6 minutes, turning over halfway through the cooking time.
6. Transfer to a plate.
7. Top the cutlets with the tomato mixture and serve.

Nutritional Information:

Calories: 237
Fat: 8.5g
Carbs: 7g
Protein: 32g

Air Fryer Cajun Tuna Steaks

Servings: 4

Ingredients:

- 1 lb. fresh tuna steaks
- 2 tbsps. Cajun seasoning

Directions:

1. Sprinkle the Cajun seasoning all over the tuna steaks and rub to coat evenly.
2. Preheat your air fryer to 400 °F.
3. Arrange the fish pieces in a baking pan, coated with cooking spray and set the timer for 8 minutes.
4. Flip the fish halfway through the cooking to brown it evenly.

Nutritional Information:

Calories: 219
Fat: 11g
Carbs: 0g
Protein: 30g

Walnut-Crusted Pork Chops

Servings: 4

Ingredients:

- 4 pork chops
- ¾ c. ground walnuts
- 4 tsps. Dijon mustard
- 1/8 tsp. salt
- 1/8 tsp. pepper

Directions:

1. Preheat oven to 360°F.
2. Apply pepper and salt to the pork chops.
3. Coat the chops with mustard and sprinkle with ground nuts until coated.
4. Arrange the chops in the air fryer basket lined with foil and cook for 20 minutes flipping over once through the cooking time.

Nutritional Information:

Calories: 309
Fat: 19g
Carbs: 3g
Protein: 33g

Cheese Almond Stuffed Tenderloin

Servings: 4

Ingredients:

- 1 lb. pork tenderloin
- ¼ c. gorgonzola cheese
- ¼ c. feta cheese
- 1 minced clove garlic
- 1 tbsp. crushed almonds
- ½ tsp. chopped onion
- 1/3 tsp. ground pepper
- ¼ tsp. sea salt

Directions:

1. Slice a pocket in the pork tenderloin.
2. Place the garlic, onions, crushed almonds, Gorgonzola cheese, and feta cheese in a medium bowl and mix well to combine.
3. Spoon the mixture into the pocket and secure it with a skewer.
4. Sprinkle the pork with salt and freshly ground pepper and place in the basket of your air fryer.
5. Preheat your air fryer to 360 °F and cook the pork for 25 minutes. Check the doneness and cook for a couple of minutes more if needed.

Nutritional Information:

Calories: 194
Fat: 7.8g
Carbs: 2.9g
Protein 28.8g

Baked Tilapia with Parmesan

Servings: 2

Ingredients:

- 2 tilapia fillets (6 oz. each)
- 2 tsps. light mayonnaise
- 2 tsps. plain yogurt
- ¼ c. shredded parmesan cheese
- 4 sprigs fresh dill
- 1 tsp. garlic powder or garlic salt, divided
- Salt and black pepper

Directions:

1. In a bowl, combine the parmesan cheese, mayonnaise, and yogurt. Line the basket of your air fryer with aluminum foil and coat with cooking spray.
2. Coat the fish fillets evenly with the prepared cheese mixture and place in the prepared basket.
3. Sprinkle with salt, black pepper and garlic pepper, top with dill leaves and slide the basket into the air fryer.
4. Cook at 400 °F for 9 minutes, until the fish flakes easily.
5. Enjoy.

Nutritional Information:

Calories: 213
Fat: 7.8g
Carbs: 2.8g
Protein: 33.1g

Zucchini, Tomato and Mozzarella Pie

Servings: 4

Ingredients:

- 3 medium zucchinis
- Sea salt
- 5 minced cloves garlic
- Freshly ground pepper
- Olive oil
- 8 oz. sliced mozzarella
- 3 sliced vine-ripe or heirloom tomatoes
- Freshly chopped basil

Directions:

1. Preheat the air fryer to 400 °F.
2. Halve the zucchini and thinly cut lengthwise into strips
3. Apply pepper and salt for seasoning and allow to sit in a colander for 9-10 minutes.
4. Transfer to paper towels to drain.
5. In an even layer, arrange the zucchini in a small baking dish and sprinkle with the minced garlic and pepper.
6. Sprinkle with olive oil and top with the mozzarella slices, followed by the tomato slices.
7. Sprinkle with the chopped basil, sea salt, and pepper.
8. Place the pan in the basket and bake at 400 °F for 25 minutes, until the cheese has melted.
9. Remove from the air fryer and let it sit for 10 minutes.
10. Serve warm and enjoy

Nutritional Information:

Calories: 195
Fat: 10.4g
Carbs: 9.6g
Protein: 18.2g

Chicken with Tomato Mixture

Servings: 4

Ingredients:

- 4 chicken breasts
- Pinch of salt
- ¼ c. balsamic vinegar
- ¼ c. olive oil
- 8 slices fresh mozzarella cheese
- 4 Roma tomatoes, seeded, diced
- 8 chopped basil leaves
- 3 minced cloves fresh garlic
- 1 tbsp. balsamic vinegar

Directions:

1. Preheat your air fryer to 400 °F.
2. In a bowl, mix ¼ cup olive oil and ¼ cup balsamic vinegar.
3. Season the chicken breasts with salt and coat with the balsamic mixture.
4. Place them in the basket lined with foil and air fry for 18 minutes, turning over halfway through the cooking.
5. 3 minutes prior to full readiness, top each chicken piece with 2 slices of cheese.
6. Place the tomatoes, 1 tablespoon balsamic vinegar, salt and garlic in a medium bowl and mix to combine.
7. Transfer the warm chicken to a serving dish, spoon the tomato mixture over and garnish with basil leaves
8. Enjoy.

Nutritional Information:

Calories: 513
Fat: 25.5g
Carbs: 7.7g
Protein 50.1 g

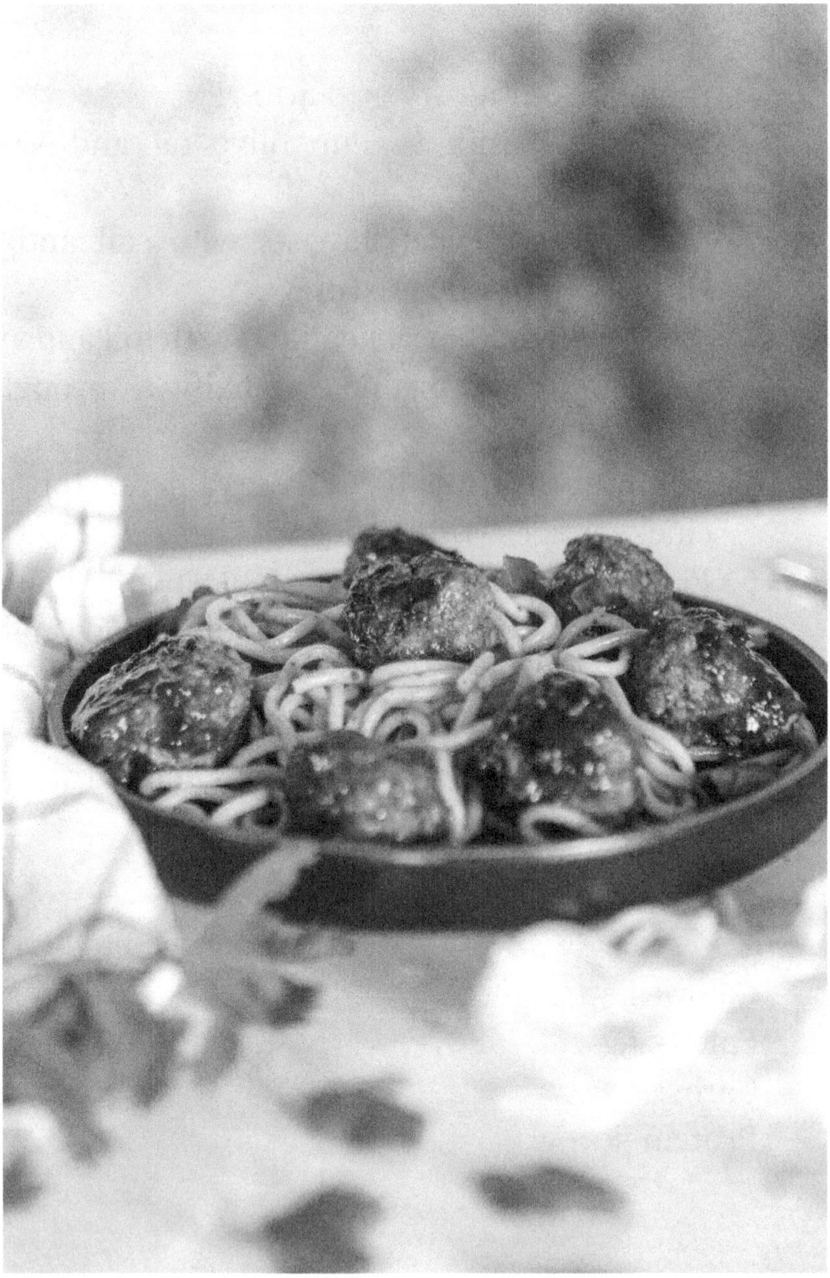

Appetizers

Breaded Jalapeno Poppers

Servings: 8

Ingredients

- 16 pcs. medium sized Jalapenos
- olive oil spray

For the breading:

- 1 c. all-purpose flour
- 2 beaten whole eggs
- 1 c. breadcrumbs
- ½ tsp. kosher salt
- ¼ tsp. ground black pepper

Directions:

1. Wash the jalapenos under running water. Dry them with paper towels.
2. In a mixing bowl, place flour then season with salt and pepper.
3. Place beaten eggs and breadcrumbs in separate bowls.
4. Coat the jalapenos in seasoned flour, and then beaten eggs, and lastly in breadcrumbs.
5. Preheat your Air Fryer to 390°F.
6. Arrange breaded jalapenos in the cooking basket such that it is not too overcrowded. Spray with oil.
7. Cook for 7-10 minutes or until breadcrumbs turns golden brown.
8. Serve hot with your favorite dipping sauce and enjoy!

Nutritional Information:

Calories: 164
Fat: 6.6g
Carbs: 23.2g
Protein: 5.1g

Sweet Potato Fries with Basil

Servings: 6

Ingredients

- 6 sweet potatoes, sliced
- ¼ c. olive oil
- 2 tbsps. chopped basil leaves, fresh
- 5g sweet paprika
- ½ tsp. sea salt
- ½ tsp. black pepper

Directions:

1. Soak the sweet potatoes in water for at least 30 minutes. Drain thoroughly and pat dry with paper towel.
2. Preheat your Air Fryer to 360°F.
3. Combine the olive oil, basil, paprika, salt, and pepper in a large bowl. Add the sliced sweet potatoes. Toss to coat well.
4. Transfer the sweet potatoes into the cooking basket and cook until browned for about 25 minutes.
5. Garnish with basil leaves.
6. Serve and enjoy!

Nutritional Information:

Calories: 221
Fat: 9.2g
Carbs: 35g
Protein: 2.1g

Red Pepper Bites with Mozzarella

Servings: 8

Ingredients

- 80g red bell pepper
- 8 oz. mozzarella, sliced
- 2 beaten eggs
- ¾ c. all-purpose flour
- ¾ c. Panko breadcrumbs
- ½ tsp. garlic powder
- ¼ tsp. kosher
- ¼ tsp. black pepper
- olive oil spray

Directions:

1. Chop off the tip and end of each red bell pepper. Make a vertical slice to open it. Remove the seeds.
2. Place a mozzarella stick in a red bell pepper shaft and then roll.
3. In a bowl, combine pepper, garlic powder, all-purpose flour, and salt.
4. Prepare ingredients by placing the beaten eggs, all-purpose flour mixture, and breadcrumbs in separate bowls.
5. Coat the red bell pepper and mozzarella roll first in flour mixture, then beaten eggs, and the Panko breadcrumbs. Spray with oil.
6. Preheat your Hot Air Fryer to 390° F.
7. Place the coated red bell pepper and mozzarella rolls in the Air Fryer cooking basket, careful not to overcrowd.
8. Cook until brown for approximately 10 minutes.
9. Serve with your choice of dipping sauce and enjoy!

Nutritional Information:

Calories: 202
Fat: 10.2g
Carbs: 19.1g
Protein: 11.4g

Air Fried Tofu with Peanut Dipping Sauce

Servings: 6

Ingredients

- 16 oz. cubed firm tofu
- 185g all-purpose flour
- ½ tsp. Himalayan salt
- ½ tsp. ground black pepper
- olive oil spray
  For the dipping sauce:
- 1/3 c. smooth low-sodium peanut butter
- 1 tsp. minced garlic
- 2 tbsps. light soy sauce
- 1 tbsp. fresh lime juice
- 1 tsp. brown sugar
- 1/3 c. water
- 2 tbsps. chopped roasted peanuts

Directions:

1. In a bowl, mix all dipping sauce ingredients. Cover it with plastic wrap and keep refrigerated until ready to serve.
2. To make the fried tofu, season all-purpose flour with salt and pepper.
3. Coat the tofu cubes with the flour mixture. Spray with oil.
4. Preheat your Air Fryer to 390°F.
5. Place coated tofu in the cooking basket. Careful not to overcrowd them.
6. Cook until browned for approximately 8 minutes.
7. Serve with prepared peanut dipping sauce.
8. Enjoy!

Nutritional Information:

Calories: 256
Fat: 14.1g
Carbs: 21.2g
Protein: 12.4 g

Tuna and Potato Croquettes

Servings: 12

Ingredients

- 4 potatoes, washed, peeled and cubed
- 10 oz. canned tuna in water, drained
- 1 whole egg
- 2 tbsps. grated parmesan cheese
- 2 tbsps. all-purpose flour
- 2 tbsps. chopped fresh chives
- ¼ tsp. kosher salt
- ¼ tsp. black pepper
- olive oil spray

For the breading:
- 1 c. all-purpose flour
- 2 beaten eggs
- 1 c. Panko breadcrumbs

Directions:

1. To start making the potato croquettes, boil the cubed potatoes in boiling water with a pinch of salt until fork tender. Then, drain in your colander and transfer to a bowl; mash using a fork. Set aside to cool.
2. Add the tuna, egg, parmesan cheese, flour, and chives in the bowl with mashed potatoes. Mix well. Season with salt and pepper.
3. Scoop about 2 tbsp. of the potato mixture and shape into small logs. Set aside.
4. Prepare the breading by placing the all-purpose flour, eggs, and breadcrumbs in 3 separate bowls.
5. Coat the potato logs with flour, then eggs, and lastly breadcrumbs. Spray with oil.
6. Preheat your Air Fryer to 390°F.
7. Arrange the potato croquettes in the Air Fryer cooking basket evenly, but not too crowded.
8. Cook until browned.
9. Serve with your favorite dipping sauce.
10. Enjoy!

Nutritional Information:

Calories: 172
Fat: 4.4g
Carbs: 27.2g
Protein: 10.1g

Beef and Vegetable Samosas

Servings: 12

Ingredients

- 4 potatoes, cubed
- 1 tbsp. ground cumin
- 1 tbsp. ground turmeric
- 1 tbsp. ground fennel seeds
- 2 chopped onions
- ¼ c. chopped serano chile
- 2 tsps. Grated ginger
- 1 tbsp. minced garlic
- ½ lb. lean ground beef
- 1 c. frozen green peas, thawed
- 1 c. minced carrots
- 1 tsp. sea salt
- ¼ tsp. black pepper
- 8 oz. wonton wrappers, large
- 1 beaten egg
- 1/3 c. olive oil

Directions:

1. Cook potatoes in a pot with boiling salted water for about 20-25 minutes or until tender. Drain and set aside to cool. Then, chop the potatoes.
2. In a skillet, cook cumin, turmeric and fennel seeds together, stirring occasionally.
3. Add in oil, garlic, onion, seranno chile, ginger, and beef. Cook until beef turns golden brown and the spices become soft.
4. Stir in peas, potatoes, and carrots. Cook for another 3 minutes. Season with salt and pepper. Mix well. Remove from heat. Let the mixture to cool.
5. Take a wonton wrapper. Place 2 tbsp. of the beef and potato filling. Fold into a triangle. Seal the wrapper with the beaten egg.
6. Preheat Air Fryer to 390°F.
7. Place samosa triangles in the cooking basket. Spray with oil. Do not overcrowd.
8. Cook until browned for 5 minutes. Cook in batches.
9. Serve with your choice of sauce.
10. Enjoy!

Nutritional Information:

Calories: 172
Fat: 4.4g
Carbs: 27.2g
Protein: 10.1g

Air-Fried Mozzarella Sticks with Sesame Seeds

Servings: 8

Ingredients

- 16 oz. mozzarella cheese, sliced
- 2 beaten whole eggs
- 165g Japanese breadcrumbs
- 2/3 c. all-purpose flour
- ½ tsp. ground coriander seed
- ½ tsp. kosher salt
- ¼ tsp. ground black pepper
- 2 tbsps. sesame seeds
- cooking oil spray

Directions:

1. In a bowl, combine pepper, coriander, all-purpose flour, and salt.
2. Prepare ingredients by placing beaten eggs, all-purpose flour mixture, breadcrumbs and sesame seeds in separate bowls.
3. Coat mozzarella sticks first in all-purpose flour mixture, then beaten eggs, breadcrumbs, and sesame seeds.
4. Preheat your Air Fryer to 390°F.
5. Arrange the coated mozzarella sticks in the Air Fryer cooking basket, be careful not to overcrowd.
6. Cook mozzarella sticks until browned for 10 minutes.
7. Serve with your choice of dipping sauce and enjoy!

Nutritional Information:

Calories: 195
Fat: 9.4g
Carbs: 19.3g
Protein: 9.5g

Zucchini Wedges with Marinara Sauce

Servings: 8

Ingredients

- 4 sized zucchini, sliced
  For the breading:
- 1 c. all-purpose flour
- 2 whole eggs, beaten
- ½ tsp. kosher salt
- ¼ tsp. ground black pepper
  For the marinara sauce:
- 2 tbsps. olive oil
- 1 tbsp. (10 g) garlic, minced
- ½ c. chopped onion
- 28 oz. canned crushed tomatoes
- ½ tsp. dried oregano leaves
- ½ tsp. dried parsley
- ½ tsp. sweet paprika

Directions:

1. Make the marinara sauce by heating olive oil a small sauce pan.
2. Sauté onions and garlic until fragrant.
3. Mix in crushed tomatoes, oregano leaves, parsley, and cayenne pepper. Stir together. Add in parmesan cheese. Turn the heat to low and simmer the sauce for about 30 minutes.
4. As the marinara sauce is being cooked. Prepare the zucchini wedges.
5. In a mixing bowl, place all-purpose flour and season with salt and pepper.
6. Place beaten eggs in a separate bowl.
7. Coat zucchini wedges first in seasoned flour and then beaten eggs.
8. Preheat your Air Fryer to 390°F.
9. Arrange coated zucchini wedges in a cooking basket without them being too crowded. Spray lightly with oil.
10. Cook until golden brown for approximately 10 minutes.
11. Turn off the burner and transfer marinara sauce into a serving bowl.
12. Serve with zucchini wedges.
13. Enjoy!

Nutritional Information:

Calories: 153
Fat: 7.4g
Carbs: 19.2g
Protein: 7.7g

Cod Fritters with Chives

Servings: 6

Ingredients

- 1 lb. flaked cod
- 3g minced clove garlic
- 1 chopped shallot
- ½ c. all-purpose flour
- 1 grated carrot
- ¼ c. chopped fresh chives
- 1 beaten egg
- ½ tsp. kosher salt
- ¼ tsp. ground black pepper
- olive oil spray

Directions:

1. Preheat your Hot Air Fryer to 390° F.
2. Mix together the cod the rest of the ingredients in a large bowl.
3. Form into small balls. Spray lightly with oil.
4. Place the cod fritters in the Air Fryer cooking basket and cook until browned for 15 minutes.
5. Serve and enjoy.

Nutritional Information:

Calories: 182
Fat: 6.7g
Carbs: 11.2g
Protein: 20.4g

Spiced Potato Chip with Garlic Yogurt Dip

Servings: 4

Ingredients

- 4 potatoes, cleaned and sliced
- 2 tbsps. olive oil
- ½ tsp. sea salt
- ½ tsp. black pepper
- ½ tsp. nutmeg, grated

For the Garlic Yogurt Dip:
- 1 tsp. crushed garlic
- ¼ tsp. sea salt
- ¼ tsp. ground black pepper
- 6 oz. plain Greek yogurt
- 1 tbsp. fresh lemon juice

Directions:

1. Preheat your Hot Air Fryer to 390°F.
2. In a mixing bowl, combine the olive oil, salt, pepper, and nutmeg. Mix well.
3. Add the sliced potatoes to mixture and toss, making sure every potato slice is coated well.
4. Arrange coated potato slices in the Air Fryer basket and cook in batches to avoid overcrowding.
5. Cook each batch for about 15 minutes or until crisp and golden brown.
6. As the potato chips are being cooked, prepare the garlic yogurt dip.
7. In a mortar and pestle, combine garlic, and salt then crushes together. Transfer this mixture into a small bowl. Add yogurt and lemon juice. Season with pepper. Refrigerate until ready to serve.
8. Once all the potato chips have been cooked, serve with garlic yogurt dip.
9. Enjoy!

Nutritional Information:

Calories: 174
Fat: 8g
Carbs: 20.2g
Protein: 6.3g

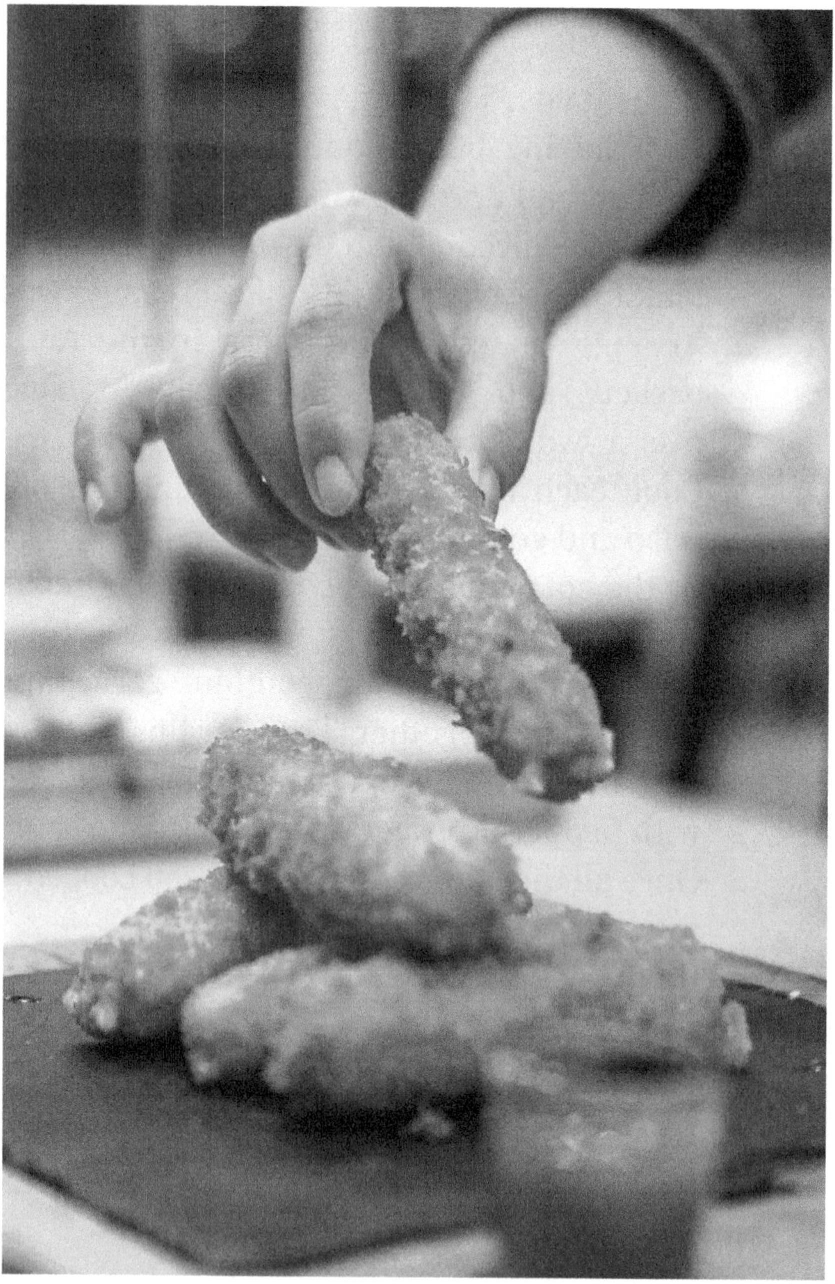

Desserts/Snacks

Bruschetta with Pesto Cheese and Tomato

Servings: 6 (2 pieces each)

Ingredients

- 1 loaf baguette, sliced crosswise into 12 slices
- 1 c. sliced cherry tomatoes
- 4 oz. mozzarella cheese, shredded
- ¾ c. prepared pesto
- ¼ c. basil leaves, coarsely chopped

Directions:

1. Preheat Air Fryer to 390°F.
2. To one side of baguette, spread pesto sauce and top with mozzarella and then with sliced cherry tomatoes.
3. Place bruschetta in the Air Fryer cooking basket and cook for 3-5 minutes. Sprinkle with fresh basil.
4. Transfer bruschetta into a serving dish.
5. Serve and enjoy!

Nutritional Information:

Calories: 216
Fat: 8.2g
Carbs: 27g
Protein: 9g

Air Fried Pumpkin Chips

Servings: 6

Ingredients

- 1½ lbs. pumpkin, peeled
- 3 tbsps. olive oil
- ½ tsp. ground coriander seeds
- ½ tsp. paprika
- ¼ tsp. sea salt
- ¼ tsp. black pepper

Directions:

1. Preheat your Hot Air Fryer to 360°F.
2. Slice pumpkin into ¼-inch thick cuts and use round 2-inch diameter cookie-cutter to produce round pumpkin chips.
3. In a bowl, mix ground coriander, sea salt, olive oil, and pepper. Mix well.
4. Add the sliced pumpkin into the mixture and toss, making sure every chip is coated well.
5. Place the coated pumpkin slices in the Air Fryer cooking basket. Cook until browned and crisp in batches if needed for about 20 minutes.
6. Serve with your favorite dipping sauce.
7. Enjoy!

Nutritional Information:

Calories: 173
Fat: 8g
Carbs: 25.2g
Protein: 5.1g

Cheesy Bacon Fries

Servings: 4

Ingredients

- 2 russet potatoes, peeled and sliced
- 5 slices bacon, diced
- 2 tbsps. vegetable oil
- 2½ c. shredded cheddar
- 3 oz. melted cream cheese
- Salt and pepper
- ¼ c. chopped scallions

Directions

1. In a pot, add salted water and bring to a boil.
2. Add potatoes to the salted water and allow to boil for 4 minutes until blanched.
3. Strain the potatoes in a colander and rinse thoroughly with cold water to remove starch from the surface. Dry them with a kitchen towel.
4. Pre-heat your Air Fryer to 400 degrees F.
5. Add chopped bacon to your Air Fryer's cooking basket and cook for 4 minutes until crispy, making sure to give the basket a shake after 2 minutes. Drain the bacon and set aside.
6. Add dried potatoes to the cooking basket and drizzle olive oil on top to coat. Cook for 25 minutes, making sure to keep shaking the basket after every 5 minutes. Season the potatoes with salt and pepper after 12 minutes.
7. Once cooked, transfer the fries to an 8-inch pan.
8. In a bowl, mix 2 cups of cheddar with melted cream cheese. Pour over the potatoes. Add in crumbled bacon.
9. Place the pan into the air fryer's cooking basket and cook for 5 more minutes at 340 degrees F.
10. Sprinkle chopped scallions on top and serve with your desired dressing.

11. Enjoy!

Nutritional Information:

Calories: 447
Fat: 28g
Carbs: 44g
Protein: 5g

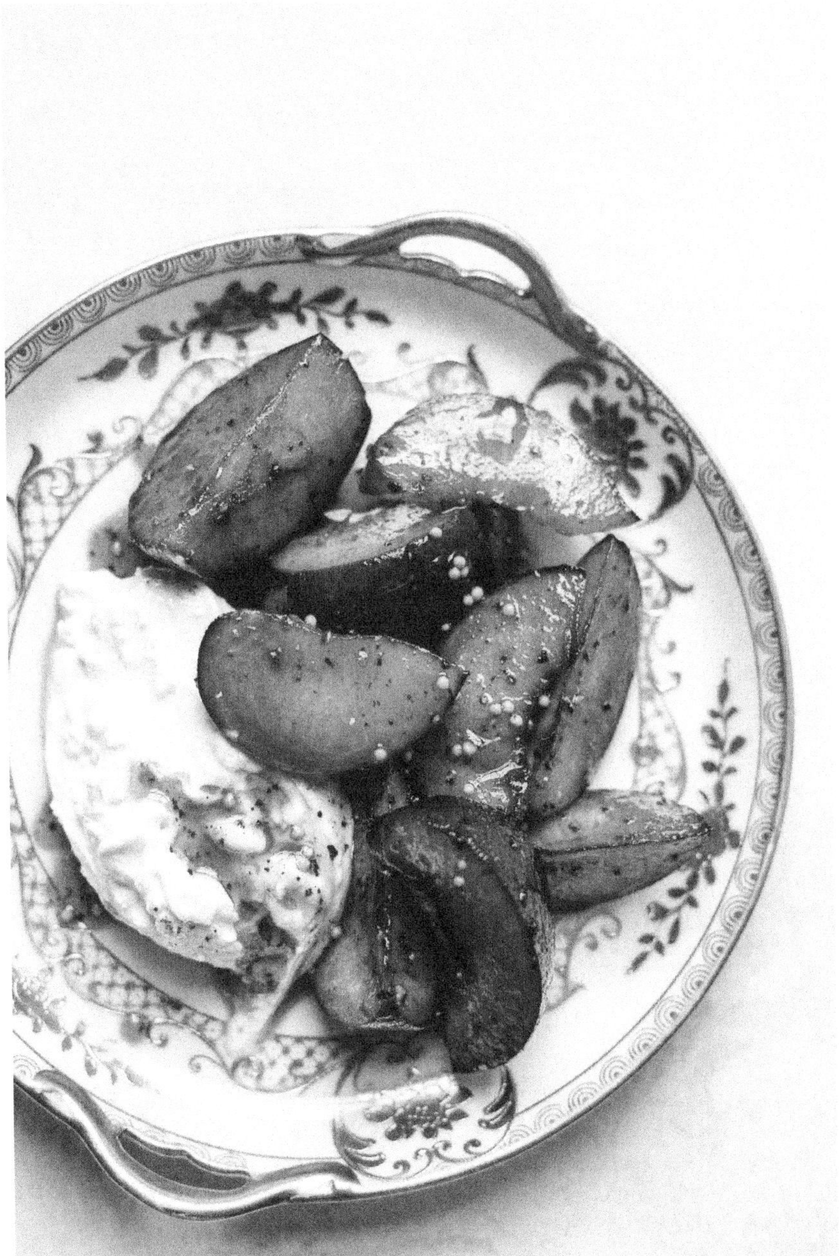

Apple Cinnamon Crumble with Almond

Servings: 6

Ingredients

For the stewed apples:
- 1½ lbs. apples, peeled, halved and cored
- 1 c. water
- 1/3 c. brown sugar
- 1 tsp. ground cinnamon

For the crumble:

- 4 oz. cold butter
- 4 oz. flour
- 3 oz. ground almonds
- 3 oz. oats
- 1/3 c. brown sugar
- 1 tsp. cinnamon powder
- pinch of salt

Directions:

1. Preheat your Air Fryer to 360°F.
2. Cut the apples into small pieces.
3. In a large saucepan, heat ¾ cup of water and bring to a simmer. Add the apple chunks, brown sugar, and cinnamon. Cook, stirring for about 10 minutes or until apples are softened and a sauce has become thick. Set aside.
4. In a food processor, process all ingredients for the crumble until combined well, and the texture turns crumbly.
5. Place the stewed apples into a baking dish that can fit into the Air Fryer cooking basket. Then, top apples with crumble mixture. Cook for 25-30 minutes, or until golden brown. Let cool.
6. Divide among 6 serving bowls.
7. Serve and enjoy!

Nutritional Information:

Calories: 334
Fat: 14g
Carbs: 51g
Protein: 5g

Peach with Cinnamon Dessert

Servings: 4

Ingredients

- 4 ripe peaches, stoned and quartered
- 2 tbsps. butter, melted
- 2 tbsps. brown sugar
- 1 tbsp. lemon juice
- 1 tsp. cinnamon powder

Directions:

1. Preheat Air Fryer to 360°F.
2. In a small mixing bowl, combine together butter, sugar, and cinnamon powder. Mix well.
3. Coat all peaches with butter mixture.
4. Place the peaches in the Air Fryer cooking basket and cook for 5-7 minutes. Cool slightly.
5. Transfer into a serving dish.
6. Serve and enjoy!

Nutritional Information:

Calories: 189
Fat: 12.1g
Carbs: 19.2g
Protein: 2.4g

Conclusion

I hope this book was able to help you to understand the benefits of an Air Fryer and the basics on how to use it. Having said that, the next step is to experiment with the different recipes. Once you have tried several recipes, you can already start tweaking the ingredients to create variations or start making your own.
Enjoy the journey!

*-- **Olivia Wood***

Made in the USA
Middletown, DE
12 September 2019